The little CHINESE cookbook

MURDOCH BOOKS

The little
CHINESE
cookbook

Contents

AN ENORMOUS COUNTRY, WITH A
LARGE POPULATION TO FEED AND A DIVERSE GEOGRAPHY
AND CLIMATE, CHINA HAS ONE OF THE GREAT CUISINES
OF THE WORLD AND EATING PLAYS A MAJOR ROLE IN
DAILY LIFE AND IN RITUALS AND FESTIVITIES.

Chinese meals always have as their basis a staple, or fan, such as rice, wheat, maize or millet. Rice, always white and polished, is the food most associated with China and is usually steamed, while wheat grows well in the harsh climate of the North and is made into breads and noodles. In poorer areas, millet is more common, eaten as porridge. The staple is then accompanied by secondary dishes, or cai, of meat, seafood or vegetables, pickles and condiments. Snacks, from dumplings to spicy bowls of noodles, are eaten all day long, both as sustenance and to satisfy the taste buds.

INGREDIENTS

The most important factor is freshness: poultry and seafood are bought live, and a cook may make more than one trip to the market a day. Chinese cuisine developed around the foods available— often there was little meat, poultry or fish, so rice and vegetables are particularly important. However, many of the foods we associate with

China today, such as chillies, capsicums (peppers) and corn, all came to China via trading routes. The Chinese also incorporate a lot of preserved vegetables and dried foods, particularly seafood, into their diet, which is especially important in areas where the climate and terrain make growing enough food a struggle.

FLAVOURS

Chinese cooking tries to reach a balance between tastes: sweet and sour, hot and cold, plain and spicy. At the heart of Chinese food is a trinity of flavours: ginger, spring onions (scallions) and garlic. Although these are not included in all Chinese dishes, they do contribute to a flavour that is seen as being quintessentially 'Chinese'. Soya bean products are another essential ingredient, and fermented tofu, soy sauce and bean sauces are tastes that define Chinese food, along with vinegars and sesame oil. In the West of the country, chilli and Sichuan pepper add heat to ingredients that are usually more simply cooked.

COOKING STYLES

A wok is without doubt the central item in a Chinese kitchen, and wok cooking, either stir-frying or deep-frying, is at the heart of China's quick style of cooking. Other techniques, such as steaming, poaching and braising, cook food more slowly. Few families own an oven, and foods that need to be oven-roasted, such as roast ducks or char siu, are instead bought from special restaurants. All food is 'prepared' in China, where salads and raw foods are not eaten, and ingredients are cooked, however briefly, or preserved. A good Chinese meal will include a mix of cooking styles so all the dishes can be ready at the same time.

EATING

A Chinese meal will also consist of a number of dishes, all made to share, that are fully prepared in the kitchen (not even carving is done at the table) and can be picked up and eaten with chopsticks. All the ingredients must be fresh and the finished food served immediately. Stir-fried dishes should still have 'wok hei' or the breath of the wok about them, indicating they have been cooked at exactly the right heat with exactly the right timing and have been served at once.

BANQUET FOOD

Food eaten at banquets is created to be the very opposite of the everyday diet of grains. The point of a banquet is eating for pleasure, not sustenance, therefore rice or noodles are served only at the end, and may be left untouched. Banquet food is often symbolic and as extravagant as can be afforded with dishes such as abalone, shark's fin and whole fish.

MEDICAL

In no other cuisine is the medicinal nature of food so tied to everyday cooking. Achieving balance at every meal is an essential part of Chinese cooking. Every ingredient is accorded a nature—hot, warm, cool and neutral—and a flavour—sweet, sour, bitter, salty and pungent—and these are matched to a person's imbalances: a cooling food for a fever, warming food after childbirth. As well as the use of everyday ingredients, there is the custom of using exotic foods, such as dried lizards, wolf berries and black silky chickens, often cooked in special soups and preparations.

THE FOOD OF THE NORTH

The cuisine of the North, with Beijing at its centre, comes from an area that is generally inhospitable with, apart from Shandong, little fertile land, harsh long winters and short scorching summers. Historically, the region has swung between drought and flooding from the Yellow River, 'China's Sorrow', though dams and irrigation schemes have improved things in recent years. The main crops have therefore always been hardy ones: wheat and millet are eaten as noodles, breads and porridge, while in the winter, vegetables such as turnips and cabbage are supplied to the capital by farmers from neighbouring provinces, who drive in trucks to Beijing's markets and live on them until their load of vegetables has been sold. Shandong, on the coast, is the most fertile area and it has become a market garden of fruit and vegetables for the capital, as well as providing plentiful seafood.

Flavours are strong, with salty bean pastes and soy sauces, vinegar, spring onions (scallions) and garlic

all being important ingredients. Winter vegetables are preserved or pickled, while spicy or piquant condiments are eaten with bowls of steaming noodles or rice when little else is available.

The main outside influence on the region has been the Muslim cooking of the Mongol and Manchu invaders who crossed the Great Wall from the North. Mutton and, in spring and summer, lamb, is sold as barbecued skewers on the street and stir-fried and wrapped in wheat pancakes. Steaming Mongolian hotpots and Mongolian barbecues cooked on a grill are seen everywhere.

Peking Duck, however, remains Beijing's most famous dish, and is cooked in specialist restaurants all over the city. Beggar's chicken is another local speciality, wrapped in lotus leaves and clay and baked for hours in hot ashes.

In stark contrast to the warming dumplings and hotpots of Beijing's streets is the imperial cuisine created inside the Forbidden City. The presence of the court not only encouraged a huge diversity of cooking styles in the city from every province in China, but also elevated cooking to a standard

probably never seen elsewhere in the world. Food was as important to the myth surrounding the Emperor as his armies, and he employed hundreds if not thousands in his kitchens. This elaborate cuisine is no longer reproduced in its entirety, but is remembered as a set of skills, recipes and flavour combinations important today in both banquet and everyday cooking.

THE FOOD OF THE EAST
Though the huge port city of Shanghai now dominates the East, the city is very much a modern one and it is difficult to talk of a real 'Shanghai cuisine'. Rather, the city's food reflects that of the agriculturally rich provinces that surround it on the fertile plains of the Yangtze Delta. Together they have given this area the nickname of the land of fish and rice.

With a warmer climate than the North and an all-year-round growing season, the cuisine has been shaped by the variety of available ingredients, from rice and wheat to a whole array of vegetables—bok choy (pak choi), bamboo, beans and squash, as well as some of China's finest fish—freshwater carp from the tributaries of the Yangtze, Shanghai's infamous hairy crabs and fresh seafood from the coast. Duck, chicken and pork from this region are also considered particularly good and a cured ham from Jinhua rivals that of Yunnan.

The cuisine is based on slow-braising rather than steaming or stir-frying, and therefore has a reputation for being more oily than other regions. Shaoxing wine, an amber rice wine produced for both drinking and cooking in the city of Shaoxing, flavours many dishes, as does black vinegar from Chinkiang and ginger and garlic. A pinch of sugar is often added to balance these flavours, and it is in this region that sweet-and-sour dishes are most expertly cooked. Much of China's soy sauce is produced in the East, and red-cooking is a favoured cooking technique using a soy sauce and rice wine stock to braise the area's fine meat and poultry, which is also presented in the form of a mixed cold platter that begins most formal meals. Though many of the region's flavourings are strong, vegetables, fish and seafood tend to be treated simply.

The area is abundant in regional specialities, including spareribs from Wuxi cooked in soy sauce and rice wine; lion's head meatballs from Yangzhou; pressed ducks from Nanjing; and West-lake carp from Hangzhou, which also grows China's finest green tea, Dragon Well, that is sometimes used as an ingredient. The people of Shanghai love their seafood, particularly the freshwater hairy crabs so associated with the city, and available for little over a month every autumn.

Snacking is an obsession, especially in Shanghai, with jiaozi, steamed buns and noodle dishes found everywhere. While rice is grown in the region, filling wheat-based breads, dumplings and noodles are favoured, particularly in winter.

THE FOOD OF THE WEST
The cooking of China's central and western heartlands is dominated by the spice of Sichuan, whose fertile plains are fed by the Yangtze River and its tributaries. It is famous for its hot cuisine

and the sheer variety of its cooking styles, summed up in the phrase 'one hundred dishes and one hundred flavours'.

Chillies are not indigenous to China, and in fact came to Asia from South America with the Portuguese. It was therefore probably Buddhist traders and missionaries from the West who brought such ingredients and cooking techniques into Sichuan, and also left the legacy of an imaginative Buddhist vegetarian cuisine.

Sichuan pepper is the dominant spice in many dishes. Not related to Western black and white pepper, it is hot and pungent, leaving a numb sensation in the mouth. The use of chilli peppers and ginger adds additional layers of heat. Red (chilli) oil, sesame oil, various bean pastes and vinegars are common, as are nuts and sesame seeds in dishes like bang bang chicken. These flavours are uniquely Sichuanese, and are quite different from those in the rest of China.

Cooking styles are also unusual. 'Fish flavoured' (Yuxiang) sauces are made from ginger, garlic, vinegar, chilli and spring onions (scallions), usually served with vegetables like eggplant (aubergine), but never with even a hint of fish present. Other tastes include hot-and-sour (Cuan La), such as in the famous soup, and a numb-chilli flavour (Ma La), such as in the tofu dish ma po dofu with its fiery sauce. Sichuan also has its own version of the hotpot, the Chongqing hotpot, which is a heavily flavoured mix of chilli and oil and, true to the style of the region, is red-hot.

Chilli is widely used in other areas of the West, particularly in neighbouring Hunan and in Guangxi, whose Guilin chilli sauce is eaten all over China. Guangxi is also a major rice-growing region, with vast stepped terraces covering its hills.

Southwest China has the most varied mix of ethnic minorities in the country, and is the only area in which dairy products such as goat's cheese are used. Muslim influences are also apparent and goat's meat and dried beef are available. Yunnan ham is a whole ham cured in a sweetish style, and Yunnan specialities include steampot chicken, cooked with medicinal ingredients, and crossing-the-bridge noodles, cooked in a bowl of boiling hot broth.

THE FOOD OF THE SOUTH

The food of the South, and especially that of Guangdong (Canton), is renowned both within and outside China as the country's finest. Guangdong has a subtropical climate that sustains rice crops and many vegetables and fruit virtually all year round, while an extensive coastline and inland waterways provide the freshest fish and shellfish.

The area also prides itself on its well-trained chefs, whose restaurants have always catered to the rich merchants of Guangzhou and Hong Kong. They insist on high-quality ingredients, which they cook in numerous ways: stir fried, steamed or boiled, but which are usually kept simple and cooked with little oil to enhance the food's fresh flavour.

The flavours of the South are relatively simple, emphasising the freshness of the food with just a delicate base of ginger, garlic and spring onions (scallions). Unlike the rest of China, spicy or fragrant condiments are often served with dishes, particularly sauces such as soy and chilli, so the diners can add their own flavourings. The area is responsible for the invention of oyster, hoi sin, black bean and XO sauces.

Guangzhou is known for its wonderful fish and seafood dishes, served in every restaurant. Always fresh, the customer picks from a large fish tank and specifies the cooking technique. The favoured meat of the South is without a doubt pork—often roasted or barbecued (char siu) and bought from the take-away counters of roast-meat restaurants, who hang up their wares to tempt in customers. Ducks are another favourite, bred all over the South and roasted until crispy. Dim sum is a speciality of Guangzhou and Hong Kong and

these snacks, served in tea houses or dim sum restaurants, are universally popular.

The Cantonese are also known for eating just about anything—from shark's fin and snakes to monkeys and dogs. The people of this region are certainly knowledgeable and adventurous about food, though many of the more esoteric ingredients are served only at specialized restaurants or are eaten mostly for their medicinal qualities.

As well as the Cantonese cooking of Guangdong, the South is also home to the food of the Hakka people, China's gypsies, whose cooking is an earthier version of Cantonese, and Chiu Chow food from the East coast of the province, with its emphasis on seafood, goose and sauces. There are also specialities from Fujian and Taiwan.

Chapter 1

THE TEA HOUSE

Tea has been popular in China since at least the sixth century BC, and it was from China that tea travelled to Japan, Europe and India. Integral to festivals, a sign of hospitality, a medicine, and steeped in tradition, tea is both a drink and a part of Chinese culture itself.

Jiaozi

Perhaps no other food typifies the hearty characteristics of Northern home-style cooking more than these meat dumplings. You can buy good-quality wheat dumpling wrappers at Chinese grocers, which makes these a quick, easy snack to prepare.

FILLING
300 g (11 oz) Chinese cabbage, finely chopped
1 teaspoon salt
450 g (1 lb) minced (ground) pork
100 g (3½ oz/3 bunches) Chinese garlic chives,
   finely chopped
2½ tablespoons light soy sauce

1 tablespoon Shaoxing rice wine
2 tablespoons roasted sesame oil
1 tablespoon finely chopped ginger
1 tablespoon cornflour (cornstarch)

50 round wheat dumpling wrappers
red rice vinegar or a dipping sauce (page 182)

To make the filling, put the cabbage and salt in a bowl and toss lightly to combine. Leave for 30 minutes. Squeeze all the water from the cabbage and put the cabbage in a large bowl. Add the pork, garlic chives, soy sauce, rice wine, sesame oil, ginger and cornflour. Stir until combined and drain off any excess liquid.

Place a heaped teaspoon of the filling in the centre of each wrapper. Spread a little water along the edge of the wrapper and fold the wrapper over to make a half-moon shape. Use your thumb and index finger to form small pleats along the sealed edge. With the other hand, press the two opposite edges together to seal. Place the dumplings on a baking tray that has been lightly dusted with cornflour. Do not allow the dumplings to sit for too long or they will go soggy.

Bring a large saucepan of water to the boil. Add half the dumplings, stirring immediately to

prevent them from sticking together, and return to the boil. For the traditional method of cooking dumplings, add 250 ml (9 fl oz/1 cup) cold water and continue cooking over high heat until the water boils. Add another 750 ml (26 fl oz/3 cups) cold water and cook until the water boils again. Alternatively, cook the dumplings in the boiling water for 8–9 minutes. Remove from the heat and drain the dumplings. Repeat with the remaining dumplings.

The dumplings can also be fried. Heat 1 tablespoon oil in a frying pan, add a single layer of dumplings and cook for 2 minutes, shaking the pan to make sure they don't stick. Add 80 ml (2½ fl oz/⅓ cup) water, cover and steam for 2 minutes, then uncover and cook until the water has evaporated. Repeat with the remaining dumplings.

Serve with red rice vinegar or a dipping sauce.

MAKES 50

Spring Rolls

The fat, solid spring rolls found in many Western restaurants are quite different from the slender and refined spring rolls that are traditionally made to celebrate Chinese New Year. Here's an easy rendition of the classic.

FILLING
5 tablespoons light soy sauce
2 teaspoons roasted sesame oil
3½ tablespoons Shaoxing rice wine
1½ teaspoons cornflour (cornstarch)
450 g (1 lb) centre-cut pork loin, trimmed and cut into
    very thin strips
6 dried Chinese mushrooms
½ teaspoon freshly ground black pepper
4 tablespoons oil
1 tablespoon finely chopped ginger
3 garlic cloves, finely chopped

150 g (5½ oz/2 cups) Chinese cabbage, finely shredded
150 g (5½ oz/1 cup) finely shredded carrot
30 g (1 oz/1 bunch) Chinese garlic chives, cut into
    2 cm (¾ inch) lengths
180 g (6¼ oz/2 cups) bean sprouts

1 egg yolk
2 tablespoons plain (all-purpose) flour
20 square spring roll wrappers
oil for deep-frying
plum sauce

To make the filling, combine 2 tablespoons of the soy sauce and half the sesame oil with 1½ tablespoons of the rice wine and 1 teaspoon of the cornflour. Add the pork and toss to coat. Marinate in the fridge for 20 minutes. Meanwhile, soak the dried mushrooms in boiling water for 30 minutes, then drain and squeeze out any excess water. Remove and discard the stems and shred the caps. Combine the remaining soy sauce, sesame oil and cornflour with the black pepper.

Heat a wok over high heat, add half the oil and heat until very hot. Add the pork mixture and stir-fry for 2 minutes, or until cooked. Remove and drain. Wipe out the wok. Reheat the wok over high heat, add the remaining oil and heat until very hot. Stir-fry the mushrooms, ginger and garlic for 15 seconds. Add the cabbage and carrot and toss lightly. Pour in the remaining rice wine, then stir-fry for 1 minute. Add the garlic chives and

bean sprouts and stir-fry for 1 minute, or until the sprouts are limp. Add the pork mixture and soy sauce mixture and cook until thickened. Transfer to a colander and drain for 5 minutes, tossing occasionally to remove the excess liquid.

Combine the egg yolk, flour and 3 tablespoons water. Place 2 tablespoons of filling on the corner of a wrapper, leaving the corner itself free. Spread some of the yolk mixture on the opposite corner. Fold over one corner and start rolling, but not too tightly. Fold in the other corners, roll up and press to secure. Repeat with the remaining wrappers.

Fill a wok one-quarter full with oil. Heat the oil to 190°C (375°F), or until a piece of bread fries golden brown in 10 seconds when dropped in the oil. Cook the spring rolls in two batches, turning constantly, for 5 minutes, or until golden. Remove and drain on paper towels. Serve with plum sauce.

MAKES 20

叉烧包

Char Siu Bau

Mantou, or steamed buns, are a filling staple eaten all over China, but especially in the North. However, these filled, slightly sweet buns made with barbecue pork (char siu) are a Cantonese speciality, enjoyed in every dim sum restaurant.

1 teaspoon oil
250 g (9 oz) barbecue pork (char siu), diced
3 teaspoons Shaoxing rice wine
1 teaspoon roasted sesame oil
2 tablespoons oyster sauce

2 teaspoons light soy sauce
3 teaspoons sugar
1 quantity basic yeast dough (page 180)
chilli sauce

Heat the oil in a wok. Add the pork, rice wine, sesame oil, oyster sauce, soy sauce and sugar and cook for 1 minute. Leave to cool.

Divide the dough into 12 or 24 portions, depending on how large you want your buns to be, and cover with a tea towel. Working with one portion at a time, press the dough into circles with the edges thinner than the centre. Place 1 teaspoon of filling on the dough for a small bun or 3 teaspoons for a large bun. Draw the sides in to enclose the filling. Pinch the top together and put each bun on a square of greaseproof paper.

When you get more proficient at making these, you may be able to get more filling into the buns, which will make them less doughy. Ensure that you seal them properly. The buns can also be turned over, then cooked the other way up so they look like round balls.

Place the buns well apart in three steamers. Cover and steam over simmering water in a wok, reversing the steamers halfway through, for 15 minutes, or until the buns are well risen and a skewer inserted into the centre comes out hot. Serve with some chilli sauce.

MAKES 12 LARGE OR 24 SMALL

Gather in the tops of the buns as neatly as you can to make round balls. Bear in mind that they will open slightly as they cook to show their filling.

荷 叶 糯 米 团

Steamed Glutinous Rice in Lotus Leaves

Lor mai gai are a dim sum classic that also make good snacks. When steamed, the rice takes on the flavours of the other ingredients and from the lotus leaves themselves. The parcels can be made ahead and frozen, then steamed from frozen for 40 minutes.

600 g (1 lb 5 oz/3 cups) glutinous rice
4 large lotus leaves

FILLING
2 tablespoons dried shrimp
4 dried Chinese mushrooms
2 tablespoons oil
360 g (13 oz) skinless chicken breast fillet, cut into 1 cm (½ inch) cubes

1 garlic clove, crushed
2 Chinese sausages (lap cheong), thinly sliced
2 spring onions (scallions), thinly sliced
1 tablespoon oyster sauce
3 teaspoons light soy sauce
3 teaspoons sugar
1 teaspoon roasted sesame oil
1 tablespoon cornflour (cornstarch)
chilli sauce

Place the rice in a bowl, cover with cold water and leave to soak overnight. Drain in a colander and place the rice in a bamboo steamer lined with a tea towel. Steam, covered, over simmering water in a wok for 30–40 minutes, or until the rice is cooked. Cool slightly before using.

Soak the lotus leaves in boiling water for 1 hour, or until softened. Shake dry and cut the leaves in half to make eight equal pieces.

To make the filling, soak the dried shrimp in boiling water for 1 hour, then drain. Soak the dried mushrooms in boiling water for 30 minutes, then drain and squeeze out any excess water. Remove and discard the stems and finely chop the caps.

Heat a wok over high heat, add half the oil and heat until very hot. Stir-fry the chicken for 2–3 minutes, or until browned. Add the dried shrimp, mushrooms, garlic, sausage and spring onion. Stir-fry for another 1–2 minutes, or until aromatic. Add the oyster sauce, soy sauce, sugar and sesame oil and toss well. Combine the cornflour with 185 ml (6 fl oz/¾ cup) water, add to the sauce and simmer until thickened.

With wet hands, divide the rice into 16 balls. Place the lotus leaves on a work surface, put a ball of rice in the centre of each leaf and flatten the ball slightly, making a slight indentation in the middle. Spoon one-eighth of the filling onto each rice ball, top with another slightly flattened rice ball and smooth into one ball. Wrap up firmly by folding the leaves over to form an envelope.

Place the parcels in three steamers. Cover and steam over simmering water in a wok, reversing the steamers halfway through, for 30 minutes. To serve, open up each leaf and eat straight from the leaf while hot with some chilli sauce.

MAKES 8

虾饺

Har Gau

Har Gau are the benchmark dim sum by which restaurants are measured and they are not easy to make. The wheat starch dough is hard to handle and needs to be kept warm while you work with it, but the results are very satisfying.

FILLING
500 g (1 lb 2 oz) prawns (shrimp)
45 g (1½ oz) pork or bacon fat (rind removed), finely chopped
40 g (1½ oz) fresh or tinned bamboo shoots, rinsed, drained and finely chopped
1 spring onion (scallion), finely chopped
1 teaspoon sugar
3 teaspoons light soy sauce
½ teaspoon roasted sesame oil

1 egg white, lightly beaten
1 teaspoon salt
1 tablespoon cornflour (cornstarch)

WRAPPER DOUGH
170 g (6 oz/1⅓ cups) wheat starch
3 teaspoons cornflour (cornstarch)
2 teaspoons oil

soy sauce, chilli sauce or a dipping sauce (page 182)

To make the filling, peel and devein the prawns and cut half of them into 1 cm (½ inch) chunks. Chop the remaining prawns until finely minced. Combine all the prawns in a large bowl. Add the pork or bacon fat, bamboo shoots, spring onion, sugar, soy sauce, sesame oil, egg white, salt and cornflour. Mix well and drain off any excess liquid.

To make the dough, put the wheat starch, cornflour and oil in a bowl. Add 250 ml (9 fl oz/1 cup) boiling water and mix until well combined. Add a little extra wheat starch if the dough is too sticky.

Roll the dough into a long cylinder, divide it into 24 pieces and cover with a hot damp tea towel. Working with one portion at a time, roll out the dough using a rolling pin or a well-oiled cleaver. If using a rolling pin, roll the dough into a 9–10 cm (3½–4 inch) round between two pieces of oiled plastic wrap. If using a cleaver, place the blade facing away from you and gently press down on

the flat side of the blade with your palm, squashing the dough while twisting the handle to form a round shape. Fill each wrapper as you make it.

Place a heaped teaspoon of the filling in the centre of each wrapper. Spread a little water along the edge of the wrapper and fold the wrapper over to make a half-moon shape. Use your thumb and index finger to form small pleats along the top edge. With the other hand, press the two opposite edges together to seal. Place the har gau in four steamers lined with greaseproof paper punched with holes. Cover the har gau as you make them to prevent them from drying out.

Cover and steam the har gau over simmering water in a wok, reversing the steamers halfway through, for 6–8 minutes, or until the wrappers are translucent. Serve with soy sauce, chilli sauce or a dipping sauce.

MAKES 24

Food Journey

DIM SUM

*Dim sum are snacks and dumplings
that 'touch the heart' and are central
to the Cantonese tea house tradition
of yum cha. Yum cha means simply 'to
drink tea', but eating dim sum, reading
newspapers and catching up with
friends and family are all part of
the experience.*

The Chinese love to snack and each region has
its favourites, from mantou and jiaozi in the
North to little spicy Sichuan dishes. But it is in
Guangzhou and Hong Kong's tea houses that dim
sum—China's most famous snacks—are found.

Traditional tea houses are almost like a pub.
Regulars, mostly older men, spend their early
mornings sipping tea, eating just a few dim sum
and reading the newspapers. In a few tea houses,
the men are accompanied by their song birds,
whose cages are hung up around the room. Today,
most tea houses are bright, dim sum palaces.
Often huge, multi-level restaurants, they work at a
frantic, noisy pace, with office workers or families
eating a whole meal of dim sum.

Dim sum is usually eaten mid-morning, but it can be found at any time, and even enjoyed as a midnight snack in busy Hong Kong. The meal begins by choosing a tea, usually pu'er (a black tea), jasmine or chrysanthemum. In fact, yum cha is the only meal where the tea is drunk with the food rather than before or afterwards. Anyone from the table can top up the tea cups during the meal, and they are thanked by tapping your fingers on the table, expressing gratitude even when mouths are full. To get the pot refilled, the lid is lifted to the side so the waiters can see that it is empty.

Sometimes dim sum is ordered from a menu, but in the most busy places it is usually taken around the tables in trays or trolleys hot from the kitchen. Servers shout out the name of the dishes they have and people lift up the lids to peak at what is on offer. There may also be 'stations' where noodles are fried and vegetables cooked. Dim sum mostly come in small steamers or dishes, usually three servings to a portion.

Dim sum are rarely made at home and restaurants prize their chefs, who make everything by hand. These chefs undergo an apprenticeship of 3 years, and take another 5 years on average to become fully qualified dim sum chefs.

Turnip Cake

One of the more common dim sum, turnip cake is sold by women pushing hot plates on trolleys. Each portion of the turnip cake is freshly fried to order. Serve with light soy sauce or a chilli sauce for dipping.

900 g (2 lb) Chinese turnip, grated
30 g (1 oz) dried shrimp
20 g (¾ oz/2 cups) dried Chinese mushrooms
150 g (5½ oz) Chinese sausage (lap cheong)
1 tablespoon oil
3 spring onions (scallions), thinly sliced

3 teaspoons sugar
3 teaspoons Shaoxing rice wine
¼ teaspoon freshly ground white pepper
2 tablespoons finely chopped coriander (cilantro)
290 g (10¼ oz/1⅔ cups) rice flour
oil for frying

Place the turnip in a large bowl and cover with boiling water for 5 minutes. Drain, reserving any liquid, then leave the turnip to drain in a colander. When it is cool enough to handle, squeeze out any excess liquid. Place in a large bowl.

Soak the dried shrimp in boiling water for 1 hour, then drain, adding any soaking liquid to the reserved turnip liquid.

Soak the dried mushrooms in boiling water for 30 minutes, then drain, adding any soaking liquid to the reserved turnip liquid. Squeeze out any excess water from the mushrooms. Remove and discard the stems and finely dice the caps.

Place the sausage on a plate in a steamer. Cover and steam over simmering water in a wok for 10 minutes, then finely dice it.

Heat a wok over high heat, add the oil and heat until very hot. Stir-fry the sausage for 1 minute,

then add the shrimp and mushrooms and stir-fry for 2 minutes, or until fragrant. Add the spring onion, sugar, rice wine and pepper, then add the turnip, coriander and rice flour and toss to combine. Add 500 ml (17 fl oz/2 cups) of the reserved liquid. Mix well.

Place the mixture in a greased and lined 25 cm (10 inch) square cake tin (or in two smaller tins if your steamers are small). Place the tin in a steamer. Cover and steam over simmering water in a wok for 1¼–1½ hours, or until firm, replenishing with boiling water during cooking. Remove the tin and cool in the fridge overnight. Take the cake from the tin and cut into 5 cm (2 inch) squares that are 1 cm (½ inch) thick.

Heat a wok over high heat, add 2 tablespoons of the oil and heat until very hot. Cook the turnip cakes in batches, adding more oil between batches if necessary, until golden and crispy.

MAKES 6

Tofu Rolls

These delicate rolls make a change to spring rolls and are often served as dim sum. Tofu skins can be purchased either vacuum-packed and ready to use, or dried. The dried tofu skins need to be handled carefully as they break easily.

4 dried Chinese mushrooms
100 g (3½ oz) fresh or canned bamboo shoots, rinsed and drained
1 small carrot
3 tablespoons oil
300 g (10½ oz) firm tofu, drained and diced
200 g (7 oz) bean sprouts
½ teaspoon salt

½ teaspoon sugar
2 spring onions (scallions), finely shredded
1 tablespoon light soy sauce
1 teaspoon roasted sesame oil
1 tablespoon plain (all-purpose) flour
12 sheets soft or dried tofu skins
oil for deep-frying
red rice vinegar, soy sauce or a dipping sauce (page 182)

Soak the dried mushrooms in boiling water for 30 minutes, then drain and squeeze out any excess water. Remove and discard the stems and finely shred the caps. Cut the bamboo shoots and carrot into thin strips about the size of the bean sprouts.

Heat a wok over high heat, add the oil and heat until very hot. Stir-fry the carrot, tofu and bean sprouts for 1 minute. Add the mushrooms and bamboo shoots, toss, then add the salt, sugar and spring onion. Stir-fry for 1 minute, then add the soy sauce and sesame oil, and blend well. Remove the mixture from the wok and drain off the excess liquid. Leave to cool. Combine the flour with a little cold water to make a paste.

If you are using dried tofu skins, soak them in cold water until they are soft. Peel off a sheet of tofu skin and trim to a 15 x 18 cm (6 x 7 inch) rectangle. Place 2 tablespoons of the filling at one end of the skin, and roll up to make a neat parcel, folding the sides in as you roll. Brush the skin with some of the flour paste to seal the flap firmly. Repeat with the remaining tofu skins and filling.

Fill a wok one-quarter full of oil. Heat the oil to 180°C (350°F), or until a piece of bread fries golden brown in 15 seconds when dropped in the oil. Cook the rolls in batches for 3–4 minutes, or until golden. Serve with some red rice vinegar, soy sauce or a dipping sauce.

MAKES 12

The tofu skins are rather thin and need to be handled carefully as they break easily. Spread them out well before you roll them up.

Siu Mai

Some siu mai purists consider the addition of seafood to the traditional all-meat filling to be outrageous. However, the prawns (shrimp) add depth and contrast to the flavour of the pork and it is now common practice in dim sum kitchens.

FILLING
180 g (6 oz) prawns (shrimp)
80 g (2¾ oz/½ cup) peeled water chestnuts
450 g (1 lb) minced (ground) pork
2 tablespoons light soy sauce
1½ tablespoons Shaoxing rice wine
2 teaspoons roasted sesame oil
¼ teaspoon freshly ground black pepper

2 tablespoons finely chopped ginger
1 spring onion (scallion), finely chopped
1 egg white, lightly beaten
2 tablespoons cornflour (cornstarch)

30 square or round egg dumpling wrappers
1 tablespoon shrimp roe (optional)
dipping sauce (page 182)

To make the filling, peel and devein the prawns. Place in a tea towel and squeeze out as much moisture as possible, then roughly chop.

Blanch the water chestnuts in a pan of boiling water for 1 minute, then refresh in cold water. Drain, pat dry and roughly chop them. Place the prawns, water chestnuts, minced pork and the remaining filling ingredients in a large bowl and stir until well combined.

Place 1 tablespoon of filling in the centre of a dumpling wrapper. Gather up the edges of the wrapper around the filling. Holding the dumpling between your thumb and index finger, lightly squeeze it to form a 'waist', while at the same time pushing up the filling from the bottom with the other hand to create a flat base. Smooth the surface of the filling with a knife dipped in water.

Place the dumplings well apart in four steamers lined with greaseproof paper punched with holes. Put a small dot of shrimp roe in the centre of the filling in each dumpling if using. Cover and steam over simmering water in a wok, reversing the steamers halfway through, for 15 minutes. Serve with a dipping sauce.

MAKES 30

Hold the siu mai firmly in your hand and smooth the surface of the filling with a knife dipped in water to prevent it sticking.

Chapter 2

HOME-STYLE COOKING

Chinese home-style cooking is generally based around rice and two, even three, filling bowls can be devoured as lunch or dinner. The small dishes that accompany this rice are seen almost as a garnish, sometimes no more than a little pickle or dried shrimp. Home cooks also prepare their own master stock from scraps which adds a unique, rich taste to their food.

Cantonese Corn Soup

This delectable soup is a Cantonese classic. You need to use a good-quality can of creamed corn with a smooth texture, or alternatively, if it is quite coarse, quickly blend your creamed corn in a blender or food processor to make it extra smooth.

250 g (9 oz) skinless chicken breast fillet, minced (ground)
150 ml (5 fl oz/¾ cup) Shaoxing rice wine
400 g (14 oz) canned creamed corn
1.5 litres (52 fl oz/6 cups) chicken stock (page 181)

1 teaspoon salt
2½ tablespoons cornflour (cornstarch)
2 egg whites, lightly beaten
1 teaspoon roasted sesame oil

Place the chicken in a bowl, add 3 tablespoons of the rice wine and stir to combine. In a large clay pot or saucepan, combine the creamed corn, stock, remaining rice wine and salt. Bring to the boil, stirring. Add the chicken and stir to separate the meat. Return to the boil and skim any scum from the surface.

Combine the cornflour with enough water to make a paste, add to the soup and simmer until thickened. Remove from the heat. Mix 2 tablespoons water into the egg white, then slowly add to the clay pot or saucepan in a thin stream around the edge of the pan. Stir once or twice, then add the sesame oil. Check the seasoning, adding more salt if necessary. Serve immediately.

SERVES 6

酸辣汤

Hot-and-Sour Soup

This soup should not contain hot chillies—the hotness comes from ground white pepper, which, in order to get a good flavour, must be very freshly ground.

4 dried Chinese mushrooms
2 tablespoons dried black fungus (wood ears)
100 g (3½ oz) lean pork, shredded
1 tablespoon cornflour (cornstarch)
120 g (4 oz) firm tofu, drained
60 g (2¼ oz/¼ cup) fresh or tinned bamboo shoots, rinsed and drained
1 litre (35 fl oz/4 cups) chicken and meat stock (page 181)

1 teaspoon salt
1 tablespoon Shaoxing rice wine
2 tablespoons light soy sauce
1–2 tablespoons Chinese black rice vinegar
2 eggs, beaten
1–2 teaspoons freshly ground white pepper
1 chopped spring onion (scallion)

Soak the dried mushrooms in boiling water for 30 minutes, then drain and squeeze out any excess water. Remove and discard the stems and shred the caps. Soak the dried black fungus in cold water for 20 minutes, then drain and squeeze out any excess water. Shred the black fungus.

Combine the pork, a pinch of salt and 1 teaspoon of the cornflour. Thinly shred the tofu and bamboo shoots to the same size as the pork.

Bring the stock to the boil in a large clay pot or saucepan. Add the pork and stir to separate the meat, then add the mushroom, fungus, tofu and bamboo. Return to the boil and add the salt, rice wine, soy and vinegar. Slowly pour in the egg, whisking to form thin threads, and cook for 1 minute. Combine the remaining cornflour with enough water to make a paste, add to the soup and simmer until thickened. Put the pepper in a bowl, pour in the soup and stir. Garnish with spring onion.

SERVES 4

Adding the egg to the hot soup forms egg drops. Pour it in an even stream.

红烧鱼

Whole Fish with Yellow Bean Sauce

Yellow bean sauce is made by pureeing soybeans that have been salted and fermented.

750 g–1 kg (1 lb 10 oz–2 lb 4 oz) whole fish, such as
    carp, bream, grouper or sea bass
1 tablespoon light soy sauce
1 tablespoon Shaoxing rice wine
oil for deep-frying
1 tablespoon shredded ginger

2 spring onions (scallions), thinly shredded
1 teaspoon sugar
1 tablespoon dark soy sauce
2 tablespoons yellow bean sauce
125 ml (4 fl oz/½ cup) chicken and meat stock (page 181)
½ teaspoon roasted sesame oil

If you do manage to buy a swimming (live) fish, then ask the fishmonger to gut it through the gills. This is harder than gutting through the stomach, but leaves the fish looking whole. If you are gutting the fish yourself, make a cut from the throat to the tail and pull out the guts through the stomach. Remove any scales with a fish scaler or the back of a knife. Check that the gills have been cut out, then rinse the fish under cold, running water and drain thoroughly in a colander.

Diagonally score both sides of the fish, cutting through as far as the bone at intervals of 2 cm (¾ inch). Place the fish in a shallow dish with the light soy sauce and rice wine and leave to marinate for 10–15 minutes, then drain off any liquid, reserving the marinade. Fill a wok one-quarter full of oil. Heat the oil to 190°C (375°F), or until a piece of bread fries golden brown in 10 seconds when dropped in the oil. Holding the fish by its tail, gently and carefully lower it into the oil, bending the body so that the cuts open up. Cook for 5 minutes, or until golden brown, tilting the wok so that the entire fish is cooked in the oil. Remove and drain on paper towels and keep warm in a low oven. Pour the oil from the wok, leaving 1½ tablespoons.

Reheat the reserved oil over high heat until very hot. Add the ginger, spring onion, sugar, dark soy sauce, yellow bean sauce and reserved marinade. Stir for a few seconds, add the stock, bring to the boil and add the fish. Cook for 4–5 minutes, basting constantly and turning the fish once after 2 minutes. Turn the fish over and sprinkle with the sesame oil. Serve with the sauce poured over.

SERVES 4

Carefully lower the whole fish into the hot oil. If you like you can gently hold the fish open with a fish slice so the oil can get inside the cavity easily.

熏鱼

Smoked Fish

In fact, the fish in this dish is not smoked at all. Instead it acquires a smoky flavour from being marinated and braised in a spicy sauce, then being deep-fried and marinated in the sauce once more before serving.

2 tablespoons light soy sauce
1 tablespoon dark soy sauce
3 tablespoons Shaoxing rice wine
2 tablespoons rock (lump) sugar
2 teaspoons five-spice powder
1 spring onion (scallion), finely chopped
2 teaspoons finely chopped ginger

450 g (1 lb) firm white fish fillets, such as haddock,
    monkfish or sea bass, skin on
310 ml (10¾ fl oz/1¼ cups) chicken and meat stock
    (page 181)
oil for deep-frying
coriander (cilantro) leaves

Mix together the soy sauces, rice wine, sugar, five-spice powder, spring onion and ginger. Pat dry the fish and leave in the marinade for 1 hour. Transfer the fish and marinade to a clay pot or saucepan. Add the stock and bring to the boil. Reduce the heat and simmer gently for 10 minutes, or until the fish is cooked through, then drain the fish, reserving the marinade.

Fill a wok one-quarter full of oil. Heat the oil to 190°C (375°F), or until a piece of bread fries golden brown in 10 seconds when dropped in

the oil. Carefully cook the fish in batches for 3–4 minutes, or until golden and crisp (it will spit a little). Remove the fish from the oil and return it to the marinade. Leave to cool for 2–3 hours.

Remove the fish from the marinade and leave to dry for a few minutes. Cut the fish into thin slices and serve cold, sprinkled with coriander leaves.

The marinade can be reused as a 'Master Sauce' (see page 187).

SERVES 6

麻婆豆腐

Ma Po Tofu

A quintessential Sichuanese dish, supposedly named after an old woman who served this in her restaurant and whose pockmarked complexion led to the dish being called ma po tofu, 'pockmarked grandmother's tofu'. Soft tofu is traditionally used.

750 g (1 lb 10 oz) soft or firm tofu, drained
250 g (9 oz) minced (ground) beef or pork
2 tablespoons dark soy sauce
1½ tablespoons Shaoxing rice wine
½ teaspoon roasted sesame oil
2 teaspoons Sichuan peppercorns
1 tablespoon oil
2 spring onions (scallions), finely chopped

2 garlic cloves, finely chopped
2 teaspoons finely chopped ginger
1 tablespoon chilli bean paste (toban jiang), or to taste
250 ml (9 fl oz/1 cup) chicken and meat stock
   (page 181)
1½ teaspoons cornflour (cornstarch)
1 spring onion (scallion), finely shredded

Cut the tofu into cubes. Place the meat in a bowl with 2 teaspoons of the soy sauce, 2 teaspoons of the rice wine and the sesame oil, and toss lightly. Dry-fry the peppercorns in a wok or pan until brown and aromatic, then crush lightly.

Heat a wok over high heat, add the oil and heat until very hot. Stir-fry the meat until browned, chopping to separate the pieces. Remove the meat with a wire sieve or slotted spoon and heat the oil until any liquid from the meat has evaporated. Add the spring onion, garlic and ginger and stir-fry for 10 seconds, or until fragrant. Add the chilli bean paste and stir-fry for 5 seconds.

Combine the stock with the remaining soy sauce and rice wine. Add to the wok, bring to the boil, then add the tofu and meat. Return to the boil, reduce the heat to medium and cook for 5 minutes, or until the sauce has reduced by a quarter. If you are using soft tofu, do not stir or it will break up.

Combine the cornflour with enough water to make a paste, add to the sauce and simmer until thickened. Season if necessary. Serve sprinkled with the spring onion and Sichuan peppercorns.

SERVES 6

Fresh tofu and chilli pastes are readily available at markets in China.

宫保鸡丁

Kung Pao Chicken

Kung pao is one of the most classic hot-and-sour Sichuanese sauces, and can be stir-fried with seafood, pork or vegetables as well as chicken. The seasonings are fried in oil over high heat, intensifying the spiciness and flavouring the oil.

350 g (12 oz) skinless chicken breast fillet
3 tablespoons light soy sauce
3 tablespoons Shaoxing rice wine
2 teaspoons roasted sesame oil
1 tablespoon cornflour (cornstarch)
120 g (4¼ oz/¾ cup) peeled water chestnuts
3 tablespoons oil
450 g (1 lb) baby English spinach leaves
½ teaspoon salt

3 garlic cloves, finely chopped
120 g (4¼ oz/¾ cup) unsalted peanuts
1 spring onion (scallion), finely chopped
1 tablespoon finely chopped ginger
1 teaspoon chilli sauce
1 tablespoon sugar
1 teaspoon Chinese black rice vinegar
60 ml (2 fl oz/¼ cup) chicken stock (page 181)

Cut the chicken into 2.5 cm (1 inch) cubes. Place the cubes in a bowl, add 2 tablespoons of the soy sauce, 2 tablespoons of the rice wine, 1 teaspoon of the sesame oil and 2 teaspoons of the cornflour, and toss lightly. Marinate in the fridge for at least 20 minutes.

Blanch the water chestnuts in a pan of boiling water, then refresh in cold water. Drain, pat dry and cut into thin slices.

Heat a wok over high heat, add 1 teaspoon of the oil and heat until very hot. Stir-fry the spinach, salt, 2 teaspoons of the garlic and 2 teaspoons of the rice wine, turning constantly, until the spinach is just becoming limp. Remove the spinach from the wok, arrange around the edge of a platter, cover and keep warm.

Reheat the wok over high heat, add 1 tablespoon of the oil and heat until very hot. Stir-fry half the

chicken pieces, turning constantly, until the meat is cooked. Remove with a wire sieve or slotted spoon and drain. Repeat with 1 tablespoon of oil and the remaining chicken. Wipe out the pan.

Dry-fry the peanuts in the wok or a saucepan until browned.

Reheat the wok over high heat, add the remaining oil and heat until very hot. Stir-fry the spring onion, ginger, remaining garlic and the chilli sauce for 10 seconds, or until fragrant. Add the sliced water chestnuts and stir-fry for 15 seconds, or until heated through. Combine the sugar, black vinegar, chicken stock and remaining soy sauce, rice wine, sesame oil and cornflour, add to the sauce and simmer until thickened. Add the cooked chicken and the peanuts. Toss lightly to coat with the sauce. Transfer to the centre of the platter and serve.

SERVES 6

白斩鸡

White Cut Chicken

'White cut' is a poaching method used all over China, where a whole chicken is cooked in a relatively short time in a water-based broth, then the heat is turned off and the retained heat carries out the remainder of the cooking.

1.25 kg (2 lb 12 oz) chicken
2 spring onions (scallions), each tied in a knot
3 slices ginger, smashed with the flat side of a cleaver
3 tablespoons Shaoxing rice wine
1 tablespoon salt

DIPPING SAUCE
4 tablespoons dark soy sauce
1 tablespoon sugar
1 spring onion (scallion), finely chopped
1 garlic clove, finely chopped
1 teaspoon finely chopped ginger
1 teaspoon roasted sesame oil

Rinse the chicken, drain, and remove any fat from the cavity opening and around the neck. Cut off and discard the parson's nose. Bring 1.5 litres (52 fl oz/6 cups) water to a rolling boil in a clay pot or casserole, and gently lower the chicken into the water with the breast side facing up. Add the spring onion, ginger and rice wine, return to the boil, then add the salt and simmer, covered, for 15 minutes.

Turn off the heat and leave the chicken to cool in the liquid for 5–6 hours, without lifting the lid.

About 30 minutes before serving time, remove and drain the chicken. Using a cleaver, cut the chicken through the bones into bite-size pieces.

To make the dipping sauce, combine the soy sauce, sugar, spring onion, garlic, ginger and sesame oil with a little of the cooking liquid. Divide the sauce among small saucers, one for each person. Each piece of the chicken is dipped before eating. (Alternatively, pour the sauce over the chicken before serving, but use light soy sauce instead of dark soy sauce so as not to spoil the 'whiteness' of the chicken.)

SERVES 4

棒棒鸡

Bang Bang Chicken

This classic Sichuanese cold platter is made from chicken, cucumber and bean thread noodles, mixed in a sesame or peanut sauce. The sesame dressing is the authentic one but the peanut version is also very good.

1½ cucumbers
1 teaspoon salt
30 g (1 oz) bean thread noodles
1 teaspoon roasted sesame oil
250 g (9 oz) cooked chicken, cut into shreds
2 spring onions (scallions), green part only, finely sliced

SESAME DRESSING
¼ teaspoon Sichuan peppercorns
3 garlic cloves
2 cm (¾ inch) piece ginger
½ teaspoon chilli sauce
3 tablespoons toasted sesame paste
2 tablespoons roasted sesame oil
2½ tablespoons light soy sauce
1 tablespoon Shaoxing rice wine

1 tablespoon Chinese black rice vinegar
1 tablespoon sugar
3 tablespoons chicken stock (page 181)

PEANUT DRESSING
60 g (2¼ oz/¼ cup) smooth peanut butter
1 teaspoon light soy sauce
1½ tablespoons sugar
2 teaspoons Chinese black rice vinegar
1 tablespoon Shaoxing rice wine
1 tablespoon roasted sesame oil
1 spring onion (scallion), finely chopped
1 tablespoon finely chopped ginger
1 teaspoon chilli sauce
2½ tablespoons chicken stock (page 181)

Slice the cucumbers lengthways and remove most of the seeds. Cut each half crossways into thirds, then cut each piece lengthways into thin slices that are 5 cm (2 inches) long and 1 cm (½ inch) wide. Place the slices in a bowl, add the salt, toss lightly, and set aside for 20 minutes.

To make the sesame dressing, put the Sichuan peppercorns in a frying pan and cook over medium heat, stirring occasionally, for 7–8 minutes, or until golden brown. Cool slightly, then crush into a powder. Combine the garlic, ginger, chilli sauce, sesame paste, sesame oil, soy sauce, rice wine, vinegar, sugar and stock in a blender, food processor or mortar and pestle. Blend to a smooth sauce the consistency of thick cream. Stir in the Sichuan peppercorn powder. Pour into a bowl.

To make the peanut dressing, combine the peanut butter, soy sauce, sugar, vinegar, rice wine, sesame oil, spring onion, ginger, chilli sauce and stock in a blender, food processor or mortar and pestle. Blend until the mixture is the consistency of thick cream, adding a little water if necessary. Pour into a bowl.

Soak the noodles in hot water for 10 minutes, then drain and cut into 8 cm (3 inch) lengths. Blanch the noodles in a pan of boiling water for 3 minutes, refresh in cold water and drain. Toss noodles in the sesame oil and put on a plate. Put the cucumber on top, then add chicken shreds. Pour over the dressing and sprinkle with the spring onion and serve.

SERVES 6

西柠鸡

Lemon Chicken

A popular Cantonese dish of fried chicken glazed with a tart, lemony sauce. Here the lemon sauce is home-made and unlike the gluggy sauces often served with this dish.

500 g (1 lb 2 oz) skinless chicken breast fillet
1 tablespoon light soy sauce
1 tablespoon Shaoxing rice wine
1 spring onion (scallion), finely chopped
1 tablespoon finely chopped ginger
1 garlic clove, finely chopped
1 egg, lightly beaten
90 g (3¼ oz/¾ cup) cornflour (cornstarch)
oil for deep-frying

LEMON SAUCE
2 tablespoons lemon juice
2 teaspoons sugar
½ teaspoon salt
½ teaspoon roasted sesame oil
3 tablespoons chicken stock (page 181) or water
½ teaspoon cornflour (cornstarch)

Cut the chicken into slices. Place in a bowl, add the soy sauce, rice wine, spring onion, ginger and garlic, and toss lightly. Marinate in the fridge for at least 1 hour, or overnight.

Add the egg to the chicken mixture and toss lightly to coat. Drain any excess egg and coat the chicken pieces with the cornflour by placing the chicken and cornflour in a plastic bag and shaking.

Fill a wok one-quarter full of oil. Heat the oil to 190°C (375°F), or until a piece of bread fries golden brown in 10 seconds when dropped in the oil. Add half the chicken, a piece at a time, and

fry, stirring constantly, for 3½–4 minutes, or until golden brown. Remove with a slotted spoon and drain. Repeat with the remaining chicken. Reheat the oil and return all the chicken to the wok. Cook until crisp and golden brown. Drain the chicken. Pour off the oil and wipe out the wok.

To make the lemon sauce, combine the lemon juice, sugar, salt, sesame oil, stock and cornflour.

Reheat the wok over medium heat until hot, add the lemon sauce and stir constantly until thickened. Add the chicken and toss lightly in the sauce.

SERVES 6

狮子头肉丸

Lion's Head Meatballs

This dish is so named because the large meatballs are said to look like lions' heads surrounded by a mane of bok choy (pak choi). Originally the meatballs tended to be made from pork and pork fat and were coarser in texture.

450 g (1 lb) minced (ground) pork
1 egg white
4 spring onions (scallions), finely chopped
1 tablespoon Shaoxing rice wine
1 teaspoon grated ginger
1 tablespoon light soy sauce
2 teaspoons sugar

1 teaspoon roasted sesame oil
300 g (10½ oz) bok choy (pak choi)
1 tablespoon cornflour (cornstarch)
oil for frying
500 ml (17 fl oz/2 cups) chicken and meat stock
  (page 181)

Put the pork and egg white in a food processor and process briefly until you have a fluffy mixture, or mash the pork in a large bowl and gradually stir in the egg white, beating the mixture well until it is fluffy. Add the spring onion, rice wine, ginger, soy sauce, sugar and sesame oil, season with salt and white pepper, and process or beat again briefly. Fry a small portion of the mixture and taste it, reseasoning if necessary. Divide the mixture into walnut-size balls.

Separate the bok choy leaves and place in the bottom of a clay pot or casserole.

Dust the meatballs with cornflour. Heat a wok over high heat, add 1 cm (½ inch) oil and heat until very hot. Cook the meatballs in batches until they are browned all over. Drain well and add to the clay pot in an even layer. Pour off the oil and wipe out the wok.

Reheat the wok over high heat until very hot, add the chicken stock and heat until it is boiling. Pour over the meatballs. Cover and bring very slowly to the boil. Simmer gently with the lid slightly open for 1½ hours, or until the meatballs are very tender. Serve the meatballs in the dish they were cooked in.

SERVES 4

Right: Roll the mixture into balls using the palms of your hands.

Far right: Dust with cornflour (cornstarch) to prevent the meatballs from sticking when you cook them.

酸甜肉

Sweet-and-Sour Pork

Although sweet-and-sour pork is often thought of as a Western invention, it is in fact Chinese. In the original version, the pork is light and crispy and served in a piquant sweet-and-sour sauce. If you like it with pineapple, add 320 g (2 cups) of cubed pineapple.

600 g (1 lb 5 oz) centre-cut pork loin, trimmed
1 egg
100 g (3½ oz) cornflour (cornstarch)
1 tablespoon oil
1 onion, cubed
1 red capsicum (pepper), cubed or cut into small triangles

2 spring onions (scallions), cut into 2 cm (¾ inch) lengths
150 g (5½ oz) Chinese pickles
250 ml (9 fl oz/1 cup) clear rice vinegar
80 ml (2½ fl oz/⅓ cup) tomato sauce (ketchup)
300 g (10½ oz/1⅓ cups) sugar
oil for deep-frying

Cut the pork into 2 cm (¾ inch) cubes and put it in a bowl with the egg, 75 g (2½ oz) of the cornflour and 2 teaspoons water. Stir to coat all of the pieces of pork.

Heat a wok over high heat, add the oil and heat until very hot. Stir-fry the onion for 1 minute. Add the capsicum and spring onion and cook for 1 minute. Add the pickles and toss together to combine. Add the rice vinegar, tomato sauce and sugar and stir over low heat until the sugar dissolves. Bring to the boil, then simmer for 3 minutes.

Combine the remaining cornflour with 80 ml (2½ fl oz/⅓ cup) water, add to the sweet-and-sour mixture and simmer until thickened. Set aside.

Fill a wok one-quarter full of oil. Heat the oil to 180°C (350°F), or until a piece of bread fries golden brown in 15 seconds when dropped in the oil. Cook the pork in batches until golden brown and crispy. Return all of the pork to the wok, cook until crisp again, then remove with a wire sieve or slotted spoon and drain well. Add the pork pieces to the sauce, stir to coat, and reheat until bubbling.

SERVES 4

Deep-frying the pork gives it a crispy, well-browned outside while keeping the meat inside very tender.

Food Journey

HotPot

The great nomadic tribes of Mongolia may have ruled China for a century but, perhaps unsurprisingly, they did not leave behind a particularly impressive culinary legacy. However, one dish that did catch the imagination of the Chinese, and later all of Asia, was the Mongolian hotpot. For the Mongolians, this was campsite food: mutton slices dunked into a pot of boiling water, fished out and eaten.

Today, every region seems to have created its own version of the hotpot, appealing to the Chinese love of combining food, friends and family. Diners sit around tall, charcoal-burning firepots that keep the broth hot. Meat, chicken, seafood, vegetables or tofu can all be added to the broth, though many versions pay homage to the original with a platter of thinly sliced lamb. Extras might include dips for the meat and bundles of noodles, which are added to the stock at the end, then drunk as a soup.

Hotpot is particularly popular in China's North, where mutton is seen as a good winter tonic, in the South, where the hotpots are lighter and often medicinal, and in Sichuan, in the West, where peppery Chongqing broth is so chilli-hot that it gives off a hazy steam.

蒙古火锅

Mongolian Hotpot

The hotpot was introduced to northern China by the Mongolians, but it soon became so popular that regional variations evolved. Traditionally lamb or beef is used, as in this slightly adapted version of the Northern classic.

350 g (12 oz) rump or sirloin steak, trimmed
1 tablespoon light soy sauce
80 ml (2½ fl oz/⅓ cup) Shaoxing rice wine
½ teaspoon roasted sesame oil
250 g (9 oz) Chinese cabbage, stems removed and
    leaves cut into 5 cm (2 inch) squares
1 tablespoon oil
2 garlic cloves, smashed with the flat side of a cleaver
750 ml (26 fl oz/3 cups) chicken stock (page 181)
½ teaspoon salt
30 g (1 oz) bean thread noodles
225 g (8 oz) Chinese mushrooms (shiitake) or button
    mushrooms
180 g (6 oz) baby English spinach

DIPPING SAUCE
2 tablespoons light soy sauce
1 tablespoon Shaoxing rice wine
1 teaspoon Chinese black rice vinegar
1 teaspoon sugar
½ teaspoon chilli sauce or dried chilli flakes (optional)
½ spring onion (scallion), finely chopped
1 teaspoon finely chopped ginger
1 garlic clove, finely chopped

Cut the beef across the grain into paper-thin slices. Place in a bowl and add the soy sauce, 1 tablespoon of the rice wine and the sesame oil, toss lightly, and arrange the slices on a platter.

Separate the hard cabbage pieces from the leafy ones. Heat a wok over high heat, add the oil and heat until very hot. Stir-fry the hard cabbage pieces and garlic for several minutes, adding 1 tablespoon of water. Add the leafy cabbage pieces and stir-fry for several minutes. Add the remaining rice wine, chicken stock and salt, and bring to the boil. Reduce the heat and simmer for 20 minutes.

Soak the bean thread noodles in hot water for 10 minutes, then drain and cut into 15 cm (6 inch) lengths. Arrange the mushrooms, spinach and noodles on several platters and place on a table where a heated Mongolian hotpot has been set up.

(If you do not have a Mongolian hotpot, use a pot and a hot plate, or an electric frying pan or an electric wok.)

Combine the dipping sauce ingredients and divide among six bowls. Put a bowl of dipping sauce at each diner's place.

Pour the cabbage soup mixture into the hotpot and bring to the boil. To eat, each diner takes a slice of meat, dips it into the hot stock until the meat is cooked, then dips the meat into the dipping sauce, and eats. The mushrooms, noodles and spinach are cooked in the same way and dipped in the sauce before eating. Supply small wire strainers to cook the noodles so they stay together. The mushrooms and noodles should cook for 5 to 6 minutes, but the spinach should only take about 1 minute. Once all the ingredients have been eaten, the soup is eaten.

SERVES 6

香脆牛柳丝

Crispy Shredded Beef

The origins of this dish are a bit obscure, though some claim that it is from Sichuan or Hunan, probably because it is spicy. Make sure the beef is really crispy when you fry it.

400 g (14 oz) rump or sirloin steak, trimmed
2 eggs, beaten
½ teaspoon salt
4 tablespoons cornflour (cornstarch)
oil for deep-frying
2 carrots, finely shredded
2 spring onions (scallions), shredded

1 garlic clove, finely chopped
2 red chillies, shredded
80 g (⅓ cup) caster (superfine) sugar
3 tablespoons Chinese black
   rice vinegar
2 tablespoons light soy sauce

Cut the beef into thin shreds. Combine the eggs, salt and cornflour, then coat the shredded beef with the batter. Mix well.

Fill a wok one-quarter full of oil. Heat the oil to 180°C (350°F), or until a piece of bread fries golden brown in 15 seconds when dropped in the oil. Cook the beef for 3–4 minutes, stirring to separate, then remove and drain. Cook the carrot for 1½ minutes, then remove and drain. Pour the oil from the wok, leaving 1 tablespoon.

Reheat the reserved oil over high heat until very hot and stir-fry the spring onion, garlic and chilli for a few seconds. Add the beef, carrot, sugar, vinegar and soy and stir to combine.

SERVES 4

扬州炒饭

Yangzhou Fried Rice with Prawns

This well-known fried rice dish hails from Yangzhou, a city in the East. It can be served by itself as a light meal or with soup. The secret to non-clumpy fried rice is using cooked rice that has been chilled, then left out to reach room temperature.

125 g (4½ oz) cooked prawns (shrimp)
150 g (5½ oz/1 cup) fresh or frozen peas
1 tablespoon oil
3 spring onions (scallions), chopped
1 tablespoon finely chopped ginger
2 eggs, lightly beaten
1 quantity cooked rice (page 176)

1½ tablespoons chicken stock (page 181)
1 tablespoon Shaoxing rice wine
2 teaspoons light soy sauce
½ teaspoon salt, or to taste
½ teaspoon roasted sesame oil
¼ teaspoon ground black pepper

Peel the prawns and cut then in half through the back, removing the vein. Cook the peas in a pan of simmering water for 3–4 minutes for fresh or 1 minute for frozen.

Heat a wok over high heat, add the oil and heat until hot. Stir-fry the spring onion and ginger for 1 minute. Reduce the heat, add the egg and lightly scramble. Add the prawns and peas and toss lightly to heat through, then add the rice before the egg is set too hard, increase the heat and stir to separate the rice grains and break the egg into small bits.

Add the stock, rice wine, soy sauce, salt, sesame oil and pepper, and toss lightly.

SERVES 4

蚂蚁上树

Ants Climbing Trees

The unusual name of this spicy Sichuanese dish is supposed to come from the fact that it bears a resemblance to ants climbing trees, with little pieces of minced pork coating lustrous bean thread noodles.

125 g (4½ oz) minced (ground) pork or beef
½ teaspoon light soy sauce
½ teaspoon Shaoxing rice wine
½ teaspoon roasted sesame oil
125 g (4½ oz) bean thread noodles
1 tablespoon oil
2 spring onions (scallions), finely chopped
1 tablespoon finely chopped ginger
1 garlic clove, finely chopped
1 teaspoon chilli bean paste
 (toban jiang), or to taste

2 spring onions (scallions), green part only, finely
 chopped

SAUCE
1 tablespoon light soy sauce
1 tablespoon Shaoxing rice wine
½ teaspoon salt
½ teaspoon sugar
½ teaspoon roasted sesame oil
250 ml (9 fl oz/1 cup) chicken stock (page 181)

Combine the minced meat with the soy sauce, rice wine and sesame oil. Soak the bean thread noodles in hot water for 10 minutes, then drain.

Heat a wok over high heat, add the oil and heat until very hot. Stir-fry the minced meat, mashing and separating it, until it changes colour and starts to brown. Push the meat to the side of the wok, add the spring onion, ginger, garlic and chilli paste and stir-fry for 5 seconds, or until fragrant. Return the meat to the centre of the pan.

To make the sauce, combine all the ingredients. Add the sauce to the meat mixture and toss lightly. Add the noodles and bring to the boil. Reduce the heat to low and cook for 8 minutes, or until almost all the liquid has evaporated. Sprinkle with the spring onion.

SERVES 4

Make sure you separate all the minced meat as it cooks, or it will form large lumps and not resemble ants at all.

Steamed Chicken and Sausage Rice

This warming Cantonese dish is traditionally cooked in small clay pots so there is one pot for each individual. Chinese sausage (lap cheong) tastes a little like a sweet salami, but it must be cooked before eating.

4 dried Chinese mushrooms
250 g (9 oz) skinless chicken thigh fillet
1 teaspoon Shaoxing rice wine
2 teaspoons cornflour (cornstarch)
3 Chinese sausages (lap cheong)
200 g (7 oz/1 cup) long-grain rice
1 spring onion (scallion), chopped

SAUCE
2 tablespoons light soy sauce
1 tablespoon Shaoxing rice wine
½ teaspoon caster (superfine) sugar
½ garlic clove, chopped (optional)
½ teaspoon chopped ginger
½ teaspoon roasted sesame oil

Soak the dried mushrooms in boiling water for 30 minutes, then drain and squeeze out any excess water. Remove and discard the stems and shred the caps.

Cut the chicken into bite-size pieces and combine with a pinch of salt, the rice wine and cornflour.

Place the sausages on a plate in a steamer. Cover and steam over simmering water in a wok for 10 minutes, then thinly slice on the diagonal.

Put the rice in a bowl and, using your fingers as a rake, rinse under cold running water to remove any dust. Drain the rice in a colander. Place in a large clay pot or casserole or four individual clay pots and add enough water so that there is 2 cm (¾ inch) of water above the surface of the rice. Bring the water slowly to the boil, stir, then place the chicken pieces and mushrooms on top of the rice, with the sausage slices on top of them. Cook, covered, over very low heat for 15–18 minutes, or until the rice is cooked.

To make the sauce, combine the soy sauce, rice wine, sugar, garlic, ginger and sesame oil in a small saucepan and heat until nearly boiling. Pour the sauce over the chicken and sausage and garnish with the spring onion.

SERVES 4

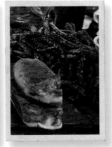

Ginger Pudding

This dessert can also be eaten as a snack. The ginger juice causes the hot milk to coagulate and forms a gingery pudding with a slippery smooth texture. It is very important to use young, sweet fresh ginger or the flavour will be too harsh.

200 g (7 oz) young ginger
1 tablespoon sugar

500 ml (17 fl oz/2 cups) milk

Grate the ginger as finely as you can, collecting any juice. Place it in a piece of muslin, twist the top hard and squeeze out as much juice as possible. You will need 4 tablespoons. Alternatively, push the ginger through a juicer.

Put 1 tablespoon of ginger juice and 1 teaspoon of sugar each into four bowls. Put the milk in a saucepan and bring to the boil, then divide among the bowls. Leave to set for 1 minute (the ginger juice will cause the milk to solidify). Serve warm.

PICTURE ON OPPOSITE PAGE

SERVES 4

Fried Fragrant Bananas

Warm, sweet and fragrant on the inside and crispy on the outside these bananas are simple to prepare and delicious to eat.

125 g (4½ oz/1 cup) self-raising flour
2 tablespoons milk
1 tablespoon butter, melted
1 tablespoon caster (superfine) sugar

4 apple or lady finger bananas, or 3 ordinary bananas
oil for deep-frying
honey (optional)

Combine the flour, milk, butter and sugar, then add enough water to make a thick batter.

Cut the bananas into 3 cm (1¼ inch) chunks.

Fill a wok one-quarter full of oil. Heat the oil to 180°C (350°F), or until a piece of bread fries golden brown in 15 seconds when dropped in the oil. Dip the banana pieces, a few at a time, into the batter and then fry them for 3 minutes, or until they are well browned on all sides. Drain on paper towels. Serve the bananas drizzled with honey for extra sweetness.

SERVES 4

Chapter 3

BANQUET FOOD

A Chinese banquet is all about conspicuous consumption. Often a huge affair, rarely held at home, it can celebrate a birthday, wedding, festival, even a funeral. The meal consists of at least eight to twelve dishes. This is by no means everyday fare, each dish must be special and special often means expensive.

极品海鲜（鲍鱼、焖荷兰和凤尾菇）

Abalone, Snowpeas and Oyster Mushrooms

Abalone is eaten in China at festival times, especially at New Year as the Chinese name bau yu sounds just like the words for 'guaranteed wealth'. Dried abalone is often used in China, but fresh or tinned abalone is much easier to prepare.

1.3 kg (3 lb) fresh abalone (450 g/1 lb prepared weight)
    or 450 g (1 lb) tinned abalone
300 g (10½ oz) snowpeas (mangetout), ends trimmed
150 g (5½ oz) oyster mushrooms
2 tablespoons oil
2 garlic cloves, finely chopped

2 teaspoons finely chopped ginger
2 tablespoons oyster sauce
2 teaspoons light soy sauce
1 teaspoon sugar
3 teaspoons cornflour (cornstarch)

Prepare the fresh abalone by removing the meat from the shell using a sharp knife. Wash the meat under cold running water, rubbing well to remove any dark-coloured slime. Trim off any hard outer edges and the mouth as well as any hard patches on the bottom of the foot. Pound the meat with a mallet for 1 minute to tenderize it, but be careful not to break the flesh.

Place the fresh abalone in a saucepan of simmering water and cook, covered, for about 2 hours, or until the meat is tender (test it by seeing if a fork will pierce the meat easily). Drain the abalone and, when it is cool enough to handle, cut it into thin slices.

If you are using tinned abalone, simply drain, reserving the juice, and cut into thin slices.

Cut any large snowpeas in half diagonally. Halve any large oyster mushrooms.

Heat a wok over medium heat, add the oil and heat until hot. Stir-fry the snowpeas and mushrooms for 1 minute. Add the garlic and ginger and stir for 1 minute, or until aromatic.

Reduce the heat slightly and add the oyster sauce, soy sauce, sugar and the sliced abalone. Stir well to combine. Combine the cornflour with enough water (or the reserved abalone juice) to make a paste, add to the sauce and simmer until thickened.

SERVES 4

Remove the meat from the abalone by severing the muscle that holds it to the shell. Trim off any hard patches.

鸳鸯大虾

Love Bird Prawns

The Chinese name for this dish, yuan yang xia, refers to Mandarin ducks known as 'love birds' because they are always seen together, symbolizing love, affection and happiness.

600 g (1 lb 5 oz) tiger prawns (shrimp)
1 tablespoon cornflour (cornstarch)
½ egg white, beaten
oil for deep-frying
150 g (5½ oz) snowpeas (mangetout), ends trimmed
½ teaspoon salt
½ teaspoon sugar

1 spring onion (scallion), finely chopped
1 teaspoon finely chopped ginger
1 tablespoon light soy sauce
1 tablespoon Shaoxing rice wine
½ teaspoon roasted sesame oil
1 tablespoon chilli bean paste (toban jiang)
1 tablespoon tomato paste (purée)

Peel and devein the prawns, leaving the tails intact. Combine the cornflour with enough water to make a paste. Stir in the egg white and a pinch of salt, then stir in the prawns.

Fill a wok one-quarter full of oil. Heat the oil to 180°C (350°F), or until a piece of bread fries golden brown in 15 seconds when dropped in the oil. Cook the prawns for 1 minute, stirring to separate them. Remove the prawns from the wok with a wire sieve or slotted spoon as soon as the colour changes, then drain. Pour the oil from the wok, leaving 1 tablespoon.

Reheat the reserved oil over high heat until very hot and stir-fry the snowpeas with the salt and sugar for 1½ minutes. Remove and place in the centre of a serving platter.

Reheat the wok again and stir-fry the spring onion and ginger for a few seconds. Add the prawns, soy sauce and rice wine, blend well and stir-fry for about 30 seconds, then add the sesame oil. Transfer about half of the prawns to one end of the serving platter.

Add the chilli bean paste and tomato paste to the remaining prawns, blend well, tossing to coat the prawns, then transfer the prawns to the other end of the platter.

SERVES 4

盐焗鸡

Salt-baked Chicken

This is a Cantonese speciality that employs a rather unusual cooking method. The whole chicken is wrapped in cloth and baked in salt, which acts like an oven, keeping in the heat to produce very succulent chicken meat.

1.5 kg (3 lb 5 oz) chicken
2 tablespoons light soy sauce
2 kg (4 lb 8 oz) sea salt or coarse salt

FILLING
1 spring onion (scallion), chopped
1 teaspoon grated ginger
2 star anise, crushed
½ teaspoon salt
4 tablespoons Mei Kuei Lu Chiew or brandy

DIPPING SAUCE
1 tablespoon oil
1 spring onion (scallion), chopped
1 teaspoon chopped ginger
½ teaspoon salt
2½ tablespoons chicken and meat stock (page 181)

Rinse the chicken, drain, and remove any fat from the cavity opening and around the neck. Cut off and discard the parson's nose. Blanch the chicken in a pan of boiling water for 2–3 minutes, then refresh under cold water and dry well. Brush the chicken with the soy sauce and hang it up to dry in a cool and airy place for a couple of hours, or leave it uncovered in the fridge.

Meanwhile, to make the filling, combine the spring onion, ginger, star anise, salt and Mei Kuei Lu Chiew. Pour the filling into the cavity of the chicken. Wrap the chicken tightly with a large sheet of cheesecloth or fine muslin.

Heat the salt in a large clay pot or casserole very slowly until very hot, then turn off the heat and remove about half. Make a hole in the centre of the salt and place the chicken in it, breast side up, then cover with the salt removed earlier so that the chicken is completely buried. Cover the clay pot or casserole and cook over medium heat for 15–20 minutes, then reduce the heat to low and cook for about 45–50 minutes. Leave for at least 15–20 minutes before taking the chicken out. (The salt can be reused.)

To make the dipping sauce, heat the oil in a small wok or saucepan. Fry the spring onion and ginger for 1 minute, then add the salt and stock. Bring to the boil, then reduce the heat and simmer for a couple of minutes.

Remove the chicken from the casserole and unwrap it. Using a cleaver, cut the chicken through the bones into bite-size pieces. Arrange on a serving dish and serve hot or cold with the dipping sauce.

SERVES 4

Stir-fried Squab in Lettuce Leaves

This dish is a Cantonese classic, sometimes called san choy bau, and the little parcels, with the contrast between their warm filling and the cold lettuce, are delicious. If squab is unavailable, chicken may be used instead.

12 soft lettuce leaves, such as butter lettuce
250 g (9 oz) squab or pigeon breast meat
450 g (1 lb) centre-cut pork loin, trimmed
80 ml (2½ fl oz/⅓ cup) light soy sauce
3½ tablespoons Shaoxing rice wine
2½ teaspoons roasted sesame oil
8 dried Chinese mushrooms

240 g (8¾ oz/1½ cups) peeled water chestnuts
125 ml (4 fl oz/½ cup) oil
2 spring onions (scallions), finely chopped
2 tablespoons finely chopped ginger
1 teaspoon salt
1 teaspoon sugar
1 teaspoon cornflour (cornstarch)

Rinse the lettuce and separate the leaves. Drain thoroughly, then lightly pound each leaf with the flat side of a cleaver. Arrange the flattened leaves in a basket or on a platter and set aside.

Mince the squab meat in a food processor or chop very finely with a sharp knife. Mince the pork to the same size as the squab. Place the squab and pork in a bowl with 2 tablespoons of the soy sauce, 1½ tablespoons of the rice wine and 1 teaspoon of the sesame oil, and toss lightly. Marinate in the fridge for 20 minutes.

Soak the dried mushrooms in boiling water for 30 minutes, then drain and squeeze out any excess water. Remove and discard the stems and chop the caps. Blanch the water chestnuts in a pan of boiling water for 1 minute, then refresh in cold water. Drain, pat dry and roughly chop them.

Heat a wok over high heat, add 3 tablespoons of the oil and heat until very hot. Stir-fry the meat mixture, mashing and separating the pieces, until browned. Remove and drain. Reheat the wok, add 3 tablespoons more of the oil and heat until very hot. Stir-fry the spring onion and ginger, turning constantly, for 10 seconds, or until fragrant. Add the mushrooms and stir-fry for 5 seconds, turning constantly. Add the water chestnuts and stir-fry for 15 seconds, or until heated through. Add the remaining soy sauce, rice wine and sesame oil with the salt, sugar, cornflour and 125 ml (4 fl oz/½ cup) water. Stir-fry, stirring constantly, until thickened. Add the cooked meat mixture and toss lightly.

To serve, place some of the stir-fried meat in a lettuce leaf, roll up and eat.

SERVES 6

木薯炒肉

Mu Shu Pork

Since wheat is the staple crop in northern China, meat and vegetable dishes are commonly served there with steamed bread or pancakes instead of rice. This Beijing dish is served rolled in Mandarin pancakes, which are first spread with hoisin sauce.

250 g (9 oz) centre-cut pork loin, trimmed
60 ml (2 fl oz/¼ cup) light soy sauce
2½ tablespoons Shaoxing rice wine
½ teaspoon roasted sesame oil
2 teaspoons cornflour (cornstarch)
5 dried Chinese mushrooms
20 g (¾ oz) dried black fungus (wood ears)
4 tablespoons oil
2 eggs, lightly beaten

4 garlic cloves, finely chopped
2 tablespoons finely chopped ginger
1 leek, white part only, finely shredded
¼ small Chinese cabbage, shredded, stem sections and
  leafy sections separated
½ teaspoon sugar
¼ teaspoon freshly ground black pepper
80 ml (2½ fl oz/⅓ cup) hoisin sauce
12 Mandarin pancakes (page 179)

Cut the pork across the grain into slices about 5 mm (¼ inch) thick, then cut into thin, matchstick-size shreds about 2 cm (¾ inch) long. Put the shreds in a bowl, add 1 tablespoon of the soy sauce, 1 tablespoon of the rice wine, the sesame oil and 1 teaspoon of the cornflour, and toss lightly to coat. Cover with plastic wrap and marinate in the fridge for 30 minutes.

Soak the dried mushrooms in boiling water for 30 minutes, then drain and squeeze out any excess water. Remove and discard the stems and shred the caps. Soak the dried black fungus in cold water for 20 minutes, then drain and squeeze out any excess water. Shred the black fungus.

Heat a wok over high heat, add 2 tablespoons of the oil and heat until very hot. Stir-fry the pork mixture for 2–3 minutes, until the meat is brown

and cooked. Remove with a wire sieve or slotted spoon and drain. Rinse out and dry the wok. Reheat the wok over high heat, add 1 tablespoon of the oil and heat until hot. Stir-fry the egg to scramble, then move to the side of the wok. Add 1 tablespoon of oil, heat until very hot, and stir-fry the garlic, ginger, mushrooms and black fungus for 10 seconds, or until fragrant. Add the leek and toss lightly for 1½ minutes, then add the cabbage stems and stir-fry for 30 seconds. Add the leafy cabbage sections, and cook for 1 minute, or until the vegetables are just tender. Combine 1½ tablespoons of the soy sauce, the remaining rice wine and cornflour, the sugar, black pepper and the meat, add to the sauce and simmer until thickened.

Combine the hoisin sauce, remaining soy sauce and 1½ tablespoons water in a small bowl. Serve the pork with the pancakes and sauce.

SERVES 4

PEKING DUCK

*Duck dishes have always been classics
of the Chinese kitchen: roasted in
Guangzhou, camphor and tea-smoked
in Sichuan, and pressed in Nanjing,
but it is in the capital that Peking duck,
perhaps China's most famous dish,
originated.*

True Peking duck must be made with a white-feathered mallard called a Peking duck. These ducks are bred on farms around Beijing and fattened up with grain for a few months to produce tender meat.

The dish is prepared in different ways by different restaurants, though there are some principles that remain the same. After the duck is plucked, air is pumped in between the skin and body to inflate the bird, then the duck is blanched in boiling water. The crispy skin is formed by washing the duck with a maltose solution and leaving it to dry in a cool, dry place. The maltose, made from fermented barley, turns a dark reddish brown when cooked to give the bird a lacquered effect.

The duck is filled with boiling water to steam it from the inside and roasted in a specially made kiln-like oven. Inside the oven, the ducks are hung vertically or spit-roasted over fruit wood at very high temperatures for a relatively short time—this produces a truly crisp skin, but prevents the meat from drying out.

The quality of the ingredients is paramount to the flavour of Peking duck. The Peking duck is specially bred to be plump and tender and is reared on a grain diet. Some restaurants add flavourings to the duck by varying the ingredients of the maltose solution or adding flavourings to the boiling water inside the cavity. However, Peking duck should not have a spicy or sweet aroma, instead the natural flavour of the duck juices and crispy skin should dominate.

Crispy skin is the true test of perfect Peking duck. This is achieved by separating the skin from the flesh, then drying the skin thoroughly before the duck is cooked. The wood-fired oven uses its high heat to cook the skin quickly, which also causes most of the fat to melt and run out, while the liquid that has been put inside the duck heats up and steams the flesh from the inside, keeping the meat moist.

北京烤鸭

Peking Duck

This dish owes its reputation not so much to the way it is cooked, but to the way it is theatrically carved and eaten, rolled into pancakes. In restaurants, the duck is cooked in a special oven, but this recipe has been modified for the home kitchen.

2.5 kg (5 lb 8 oz) duck
2 tablespoons maltose or honey, dissolved in
   2 tablespoons water
125 ml (4 fl oz/½ cup) hoisin sauce or plum sauce

24 Mandarin pancakes (page 179)
6–8 spring onions (scallions), shredded
½ cucumber, shredded

Cut the wing tips off the duck with a pair of poultry shears. Rinse the duck, drain, and remove any fat from the cavity opening and around the neck. Cut off and discard the parson's nose. Plunge the duck into a pot of boiling water for 2–3 minutes to tighten the skin. Remove and drain, then dry thoroughly.

While the skin is still warm, brush the duck all over with the maltose or honey and water solution, then hang it up to dry in a cool and airy place for at least 6 hours, or overnight, or leave it uncovered in the fridge.

Preheat the oven to 200°C (400°F). Place the duck, breast side up, on a rack in a roasting tin, and cook without basting or turning for 1½ hours. Check to make sure the duck is not getting too dark and, if it is, cover it loosely with foil.

To serve, remove the crispy duck skin in small slices by using a sharp carving knife, then carve the meat, or carve both together. Arrange on a serving plate.

To eat, spread about 1 teaspoon of the hoisin sauce or plum sauce in the centre of a pancake, add a few strips of spring onion, cucumber, duck skin and meat, roll up the pancake and turn up the bottom edge to prevent the contents from falling out.

SERVES 6

Carve the duck so that each slice has some crispy skin and tender meat. The skin can also be eaten separately, wrapped in the pancakes, while the meat is used in a stir-fry.

Mongolian Lamb

The pale green leaves of an iceberg lettuce have a refreshing flavour and their firm and crisp texture are the ideal accompaniment to the bite-size lamb pieces.

300 g (10½ oz) lamb fillet
2 teaspoons finely chopped ginger
1 spring onion (scallion), chopped
2 teaspoons ground Sichuan peppercorns
1 teaspoon salt
2 tablespoons light soy sauce
1 tablespoon yellow bean sauce
1 tablespoon hoisin sauce

1 teaspoon five-spice powder
2 tablespoons Shaoxing rice wine
oil for deep-frying
crisp lettuce leaves
80 ml (2½ fl oz/⅓ cup) hoisin sauce, extra
½ cucumber, shredded
6 spring onions (scallions), shredded

Cut the lamb along the grain into six long strips. Combine with the ginger, spring onion, pepper, salt, soy, yellow bean and hoisin sauces, five-spice powder and rice wine. Marinate in the fridge for at least 2 hours. Put the lamb and marinade in a heatproof dish in a steamer. Cover and steam for 2½–3 hours over simmering water in a wok, replenishing with boiling water during cooking. Remove the lamb from the liquid and drain well.

Fill a wok one-quarter full of oil. Heat the oil to 180°C (350°F), or until a piece of bread fries golden brown in 15 seconds when dropped in the oil. Cook the lamb for 3–4 minutes, then remove and drain. Cut the lamb into bite-size shreds.

To serve, place some lamb in the lettuce leaves with some hoisin sauce, cucumber and spring onion and roll up into a parcel.

SERVES 4

Beef with Oyster Sauce

Shaoxing wine is one of the most famous varieties of traditional Chinese wines, fermented from rice. It originates from the region of Shaoxing, in the Zhejiang province of eastern China. It may be omitted from this recipe if necessary.

300 g (11 oz) rump or sirloin steak, trimmed
1 teaspoon sugar
1 tablespoon dark soy sauce
2 teaspoons Shaoxing rice wine
2 teaspoons cornflour (cornstarch)
4 dried Chinese mushrooms
oil for deep-frying

4 slices ginger
1 spring onion (scallion), cut into short lengths
75 g (2½ oz) snowpeas (mangetout), ends trimmed
1 small carrot, thinly sliced
½ teaspoon salt
2–3 tablespoons chicken and meat stock (page 181)
2 tablespoons oyster sauce

Cut the beef across the grain into thin bite-size slices. Combine with half the sugar, the soy sauce, rice wine, cornflour and 2 tablespoons water. Marinate in the fridge for several hours, or overnight.

Soak the dried mushrooms in boiling water for 30 minutes, then drain and squeeze out any excess water. Remove and discard the stems and cut the caps in half, or quarters if large.

Fill a wok one-quarter full of oil. Heat the oil to 180°C (350°F), or until a piece of bread fries golden brown in 15 seconds when dropped in the oil. Cook the beef for 45–50 seconds, stirring to separate the pieces, and remove as soon as the colour changes. Drain well in a colander. Pour the oil from the wok, leaving 2 tablespoons.

Reheat the reserved oil over high heat until very hot and stir-fry the ginger and spring onion for 1 minute. Add the snowpeas, mushrooms and carrot and stir-fry for 1 minute, then add the salt, stock and remaining sugar and stir-fry for 1 minute. Toss with the beef and oyster sauce.

SERVES 4

Eight-treasure Rice

This Chinese rice pudding is a great favourite at banquets and Chinese New Year. The eight treasures vary, but can also include other preserved fruits.

12 whole blanched lotus seeds
12 jujubes (dried Chinese dates)
20 fresh or tinned gingko nuts, shelled
225 g (8 oz/1 cup) glutinous rice
2 tablespoons sugar
2 teaspoons oil

30 g (1 oz) slab sugar
8 glacé cherries
6 dried longans, pitted
4 almonds or walnuts
225 g (8 oz) red bean paste

Soak the lotus seeds and jujubes in bowls of cold water for 30 minutes, then drain. Remove the seeds from the jujubes. If using fresh gingko nuts, blanch in a pan of boiling water for 5 minutes, then refresh in cold water and dry thoroughly.

Put the glutinous rice and 310 ml (10¾ fl oz/ 1¼ cups) water in a heavy-based saucepan and bring to the boil. Reduce the heat to low and simmer for 10–15 minutes. Stir in the sugar and oil.

Dissolve the slab sugar in 185 ml (6 fl oz/¾ cup) water and bring to the boil. Add the lotus seeds, jujubes and gingko nuts and simmer for 1 hour, or until the lotus seeds are soft. Drain, reserving the liquid.

Grease a 1 litre (35 fl oz/4 cup) heatproof bowl. Decorate the base with the lotus seeds, jujubes, gingko nuts, cherries, longans and almonds. Smooth two-thirds of the rice over this to form a shell on the surface of the bowl. Fill with the bean paste, cover with the remaining rice and smooth the surface.

Cover the rice with a piece of greased foil and put the bowl in a steamer. Cover and steam over simmering water in a wok for 1–1½ hours, replenishing with boiling water during cooking.

Turn the pudding out onto a plate and pour the reserved sugar liquid over the top. Serve hot.

SERVES 8

Eight-treasure rice can be made in any round dish. If you want it to sit higher on the plate, then choose a deep bowl. Remember that the pattern you make on the bottom will come out on top.

桂皮牛肉面

Cinnamon Beef Noodles

In China for this recipe, cassia bark, the spice made from the bark of East Asian trees is used more often than cinnamon which is grown mainly in Sri Lanka. Cinnamon has a sweeter, more delicate flavour than cassia.

1 teaspoon oil
10 spring onions (scallions), cut into short lengths,
　lightly smashed with the flat side of a cleaver
10 garlic cloves, thinly sliced
6 slices ginger, smashed with the flat side of a cleaver
1½ teaspoons chilli bean paste (toban jiang)
2 cassia or cinnamon sticks

2 star anise
125 ml (4 fl oz/½ cup) light soy sauce
1 kg (2 lb 4 oz) chuck steak, trimmed and cut into cubes
250 g (9 oz) rice stick noodles
250 g (9 oz) baby English spinach
3 tablespoons finely chopped spring onion (scallion)

Heat a wok over medium heat, add the oil and heat until hot. Stir-fry the spring onion, garlic, ginger, chilli paste, cassia and star anise for 10 seconds, or until fragrant. Transfer to a clay pot, casserole or saucepan. Add the soy sauce and 2.25 litres (79 fl oz/9 cups) water. Bring to the boil, add the beef, then return to the boil. Reduce the heat and simmer, covered, for 1½ hours, or until the beef is very tender. Skim the surface occasionally to remove impurities and fat. Remove and discard the ginger and cassia.

Soak the noodles in hot water for 10 minutes, then drain and divide among six bowls. Add the spinach to the beef and bring to the boil. Spoon the beef mixture over the noodles and sprinkle with the spring onion.

SERVES 4

Longevity Noodles

Noodles symbolise a long life because of their length and are therefore served at special occasions such as birthdays and feast days. The noodles for this dish are particularly long and can be bought labelled as longevity noodles.

250 g (9 oz) precooked longevity or dried egg noodles
100 g (3½ oz/1 cup) bean sprouts
100 g (3½ oz/⅓ cup) fresh or tinned bamboo shoots, rinsed
1 tablespoon oil

1 tablespoon finely chopped ginger
4 spring onions (scallions), thinly sliced
1 tablespoon light soy sauce
1 teaspoon roasted sesame oil
80 ml (2½ fl oz/⅓ cup) chicken stock (page 181)

If using longevity noodles, cook in a pan of salted boiling water for 1 minute, drain, then rinse in cold water. If using dried egg noodles, cook in a pan of salted boiling water for 10 minutes, then drain. Wash the bean sprouts and drain thoroughly. Shred the bamboo shoots.

Heat a wok over high heat, add the oil and heat until very hot. Stir-fry the ginger for a few seconds, then add the bean sprouts, bamboo shoots and spring onion and stir-fry for 1 minute. Add the soy sauce, sesame oil and stock and bring to the boil. Add the longevity or dried egg noodles and toss together until the sauce is absorbed.

SERVES 4

Candied walnuts

250 g (9 oz) sugar
450 g (1 lb) shelled walnut halves

oil for deep-frying

Dissolve the sugar in 100 ml (3½ fl oz/½ cup) water and bring to the boil and cook for 2 minutes.

Blanch the walnuts in a pan of boiling water briefly, then drain. Tip immediately into the syrup, stirring to coat. Cool for 5 minutes, then drain.

Fill a wok one-quarter full of oil. Heat the oil to 190°C (375°F), or until a piece of bread fries

golden brown in 10 seconds when dropped in the oil. Add the walnuts in batches, stirring to brown evenly. As soon as they brown, remove with a wire sieve or slotted spoon and put on some foil, making sure they are well spaced. Do not touch as they will be hot. When cool, drain on paper towels. Serve as a snack or at the start of a meal.

SERVES 8 AS A SNACK

辣椒炒蟹

Chilli Crab

When preparing the crab for cooking cut the last two joints off the crab legs as these don't contain much meat.

4 x 250 g (9 oz) live crabs
3 tablespoons oil
1 tablespoon Guilin chilli sauce
2 tablespoons light soy sauce
3 teaspoons clear rice vinegar
4 tablespoons Shaoxing rice wine

½ teaspoon salt
2 tablespoons sugar
2 tablespoons chicken stock (page 181)
1 tablespoon grated ginger
2 garlic cloves, crushed
2 spring onions (scallions), finely chopped

To kill the crabs humanely, put them in the freezer for 1 hour. Bring a large saucepan of water to the boil. Plunge the crabs into boiling water for about 1 minute, then rinse them in cold water. Twist off and discard the upper shell, and remove and discard the spongy grey gill tissue from inside the crab. Rinse the bodies and drain well. Cut away the last two hairy joints of the legs. Cut each crab into four to six pieces, cutting so that a portion of the body is attached to one or two legs. Crack the crab claws using crab crackers or the back edge of a cleaver—this will help the flavouring penetrate the crab meat.

Heat a wok over high heat, add 1 tablespoon of the oil and heat until very hot. Add half the crab and fry for several minutes to cook the meat right through. Remove and drain. Repeat with another tablespoon of the oil and the remaining crab.

Combine the chilli sauce, soy sauce, rice vinegar, rice wine, salt, sugar and stock.

Reheat the wok over high heat, add the remaining oil and heat until very hot. Stir-fry the ginger, garlic and spring onion for 10 seconds. Add the sauce mixture to the wok and cook briefly. Add the crab pieces and toss lightly to coat with the sauce. Cook, covered, for 5 minutes, then serve immediately.

Crab is best eaten with your hands, so supply finger bowls as well as special picks to help remove the meat from the crab claws.

SERVES 4

新年甜汤圆

New Year Sweet Dumplings

These glutinous sweet dumplings are made at Chinese New Year and are often eaten in a sweet soup. They can be filled with a nut or bean paste.

60 g (2¼ oz) black sesame paste, red bean paste or
  smooth peanut butter
4 tablespoons caster (superfine) sugar

250 g (9 oz/1½ cups) glutinous rice flour
30 g (1 oz) rock (lump) sugar

Combine the sesame paste with the sugar.

Sift the rice flour into a bowl and stir in 185 ml (6 fl oz/¾ cup) boiling water. Knead carefully (the dough will be very hot) to form a soft, slightly sticky dough. Dust your hands with extra rice flour, roll the dough into a cylinder, then divide it into cherry-size pieces. Cover the dough with a tea towel and, using one piece at a time, form each piece of dough into a flat round, then gather it into a cup shape. The dough should be fairly thin.

Fill each cup shape with 1 teaspoon of paste and fold the top over, smoothing the dough so you have a round ball with no visible joins.

Bring 1 litre (35 fl oz/4 cups) of water to the boil, add the rock sugar and stir until dissolved. Return to the boil, add the dumplings in batches and simmer for 5 minutes, or until they rise to the surface. Serve warm with a little of the syrup.

MAKES 24

Fried Peanuts

Some form of peanut is usually in every family's Chinese New Year feast. This traditional dish is very simple to make and a great party food.

1 tablespoon Sichuan peppercorns
4 star anise
1 tablespoon sugar

1 teaspoon salt
450 g (1 lb) shelled peanuts, skins on
3 tablespoons roasted sesame oil

Put the spices, sugar, salt and 750 ml (26 fl oz/ 3 cups) water in a saucepan and bring to the boil. Add the peanuts and simmer for 5 minutes. Turn off the heat and leave the peanuts and liquid to cool.

Drain and dry the peanuts, removing the whole spices. Heat the sesame oil in a wok and fry the peanuts until brown. Serve warm or cold as a snack.

SERVES 8 AS A SNACK

Chapter 4

FROM THE WET MARKET

Wet markets are China's food stores, where local farmers congregate to sell their goods. The wet market takes its name not from the fresh nature of the goods on offer, but from the way the stallholders hose down their fruit, vegetables and fish, clearing away debris from the market and making their produce sparkle.

酸 甜 素 菜 拌 虾

Sweet-and-Sour Prawns with Vegetables

Sweet-and-sour is probably one of the most abused Chinese dishes, but when well done it can be one of the most pleasing. The key is the sauce, which has equal amounts of rice vinegar and sugar to give it its sweet-and-sour flavour.

700 g (1 lb 9 oz) prawns (shrimp)
2 tablespoons Shaoxing rice wine
2 slices ginger, smashed with the flat side of a cleaver
3 teaspoons roasted sesame oil
1½ tablespoons cornflour (cornstarch)
125 ml (4 fl oz/½ cup) oil
2 spring onions (scallions), white part only, finely chopped
1 tablespoon finely chopped ginger

2 garlic cloves, finely chopped
1 red capsicum (pepper), diced
1 green capsicum (pepper), diced
2½ tablespoons tomato sauce (ketchup)
2 tablespoons clear rice vinegar
2 tablespoons sugar
1 teaspoon light soy sauce
½ teaspoon salt

Peel the prawns, score each one along the length of the back so the prawns will 'butterfly' when cooked, and devein them. Place the prawns in a bowl and add the rice wine, ginger, 2 teaspoons of the sesame oil and 1 tablespoon of the cornflour. Pinch the ginger slices in the marinade repeatedly for several minutes to impart the flavour into the marinade. Toss lightly, then leave to marinate for 20 minutes. Discard the ginger slices and drain the prawns.

Heat a wok over high heat, add 2 tablespoons of the oil and heat until very hot. Add half the prawns and toss lightly over high heat for about 1½ minutes, or until the prawns turn pink and curl up. Remove with a wire sieve or slotted spoon and drain. Repeat with another 2 tablespoons of the oil and the remaining prawns. Pour off the oil and wipe out the wok.

Reheat the wok over high heat, add the remaining oil and heat until very hot. Add the spring onion, chopped ginger and garlic and stir-fry for 15 seconds, or until fragrant. Add the red and green capsicum and stir-fry for 1 minute.

Combine the tomato sauce, rice vinegar, sugar, soy sauce, salt and the remaining sesame oil and cornflour with 125 ml (4 fl oz/½ cup) water, add to the sauce and simmer until thickened. Add the prawns and toss lightly to coat.

SERVES 6

豉汁蒸青口

Steamed Mussels with Black Bean Sauce

Mussels are not eaten as much in China as clams, however, they are enjoyed in seaside areas. This recipe works equally well with clams if you prefer.

1 kg (2 lb 4 oz) mussels
1 tablespoon oil
1 garlic clove, finely chopped
½ teaspoon finely chopped ginger
2 spring onions (scallions), finely chopped
1 red chilli, chopped

1 tablespoon light soy sauce
1 tablespoon Shaoxing rice wine
1 tablespoon salted, fermented black beans, rinsed and mashed
2 tablespoons chicken and meat stock (page 181)
few drops of roasted sesame oil

Scrub the mussels, remove any beards, and throw away any that do not close when tapped on the work surface.

Place the mussels in a large dish in a steamer. Steam over simmering water in a covered wok for 4 minutes, discarding any that do not open after this time.

Meanwhile, heat the oil in a small saucepan. Add the garlic, ginger, spring onion and chilli and cook, stirring, for 30 seconds. Add the remaining ingredients, and blend well. Bring to the boil, then reduce the heat and simmer for 1 minute.

To serve, remove and discard the top shell of each mussel, pour 2 teaspoons of the sauce into each mussel and serve on the shell.

SERVES 4

Scrub off any barnacles from the mussels, then remove the beards (byssus) by tugging on them firmly.

海鲜沙锅

Seafood Clay Pot

A traditional, unglazed, porous clay pot will allow moisture and heat to circulate throughout the cooking process. The alkaline present in the clay also tends to neturalise some of the acids present in the food leading to a generally sweeter taste.

8 scallops
12 prawns (shrimp)
12 hard-shelled clams (vongole)
8 oysters, shucked
4 slices ginger
2 tablespoons Shaoxing rice wine

1 teaspoon roasted sesame oil
140 g (5 oz) bean thread noodles
140 g (5 oz) Chinese cabbage
1 spring onion (scallion), thinly sliced
310 ml (10¾ fl oz/1¼ cups) chicken stock (page 181)
coriander (cilantro) sprigs

Slice the small, hard white muscle off the side of each scallop and pull off any membrane. Rinse the scallops and drain. Pull off the roes if you prefer. Peel and devein the prawns. Wash the clams in several changes of cold water, leaving them for a few minutes each time to remove any grit. Scrub the clams well, discarding any that remain open. Drain well.

Put the scallops, prawns, clams and oysters in a bowl with the ginger, rice wine and sesame oil.

Marinate for 30 minutes. Soak the bean thread noodles in hot water for 10 minutes, then drain.

Cut the cabbage into small squares, put in a clay pot with the spring onion and place the noodles on top. Remove the ginger from the marinade and put the seafood and marinade on top of the noodles. Pour the stock over. Slowly bring to the boil, then simmer, covered, for 10 minutes. Stir once, season and cook for 8 minutes. Serve from the pot, sprinkled with coriander.

SERVES 4

椒盐软壳蟹

Salt and Pepper Soft-shell Crabs

These crabs are a delight to eat as you can devour the entire creature—shells and all.
They are eaten when they have just shed their old shell and before a new shell hardens.

4 soft-shell crabs
1 teaspoon spicy salt and pepper (page 183)
1 tablespoon Shaoxing rice wine
1 egg, beaten

1 tablespoon plain (all-purpose) flour
oil for deep-frying
1 spring onion (scallion), chopped
2 small red chillies, chopped

To kill the crabs humanely, put them in the freezer for 1 hour. Bring a large saucepan of water to the boil. Plunge the crabs into boiling water for about 1 minute, then rinse them in cold water. Marinate in the spicy salt and pepper and rice wine for 10–15 minutes, then coat with the egg and dust with the flour.

Fill a wok one-quarter full of oil. Heat the oil to 190°C (375°F), or until a piece of bread fries golden brown in 10 seconds when dropped in the oil. Cook the crabs for 3 4 minutes, or until golden. Remove and drain, reserving the oil. Cut each crab in half and arrange on a serving plate.

Soak the spring onion and chilli in the hot oil (with the heat turned off) for 2 minutes. Remove with a wire sieve or slotted spoon and sprinkle over the crabs.

SERVES 4

海南鸡饭

Hainan Chicken

Hainan chicken is a meal of chicken, rice and soup, eaten with a spring onion (scallion) or chilli sauce. Originally from Hainan Island in the south of China, this dish was brought to Singapore by immigrants and is now a Singaporean classic.

1.2 kg (2 lb 12 oz) chicken
2 spring onions (scallions), cut into 5 cm (2 inch) lengths
5 coriander (cilantro) sprigs
¾ teaspoon salt
4 slices ginger, smashed with the flat side of a cleaver
¼ teaspoon black peppercorns
finely chopped spring onion (scallion)

DIPPING SAUCES
2 spring onions (scallions), sliced
1 tablespoon finely grated ginger
1 teaspoon salt
3 tablespoons oil
3 tablespoons light soy sauce
1–2 red chillies, sliced

Rinse the chicken, drain, and remove any fat from the cavity opening and around the neck. Cut off and discard the parson's nose. Place the chicken in a large clay pot or casserole. Add the spring onion, coriander, salt, ginger, peppercorns and enough water to cover the chicken. Cover and bring to the boil, then reduce the heat and simmer very gently for 30 minutes. Turn off the heat and leave the chicken for 10 minutes. Remove the chicken from the pot and drain well. Skim off any scum from the liquid and strain the liquid.

To make the dipping sauces, combine the spring onion, ginger and salt in one small heatproof or metal bowl.

Heat a wok over high heat, add the oil and heat until smoking. Allow it to cool slightly, then pour over the spring onion mixture. The mixture will splatter. Stir well. Combine the soy sauce and chilli in another small bowl.

Using a cleaver, cut the chicken through the bones into bite size pieces. Pour the stock into soup bowls, sprinkle with the finely chopped spring onion, and serve with the chicken along with bowls of rice and the dipping sauces.

SERVES 4

脆皮鸭

Crispy Skin Duck

Northern chefs have their famous Peking duck, but in Sichuan, crispy skin duck is equally popular. This dish can also be made with boneless duck breasts, just adjust the cooking times. Serve the duck with mandarin pancakes or steamed flower rolls.

2.25 kg (5 lb) duck

8 spring onions (scallions), ends trimmed, smashed with the flat side of a cleaver

8 slices ginger, smashed with the flat side of a cleaver

3 tablespoons Shaoxing rice wine

2 tablespoons salt

2 teaspoons Sichuan peppercorns

1 star anise, smashed with the flat side of a cleaver

2 tablespoons light soy sauce

125 g (4½ oz/1 cup) cornflour (cornstarch)

oil for deep-frying

hoisin sauce

Mandarin pancakes (page 179) or steamed breads

Rinse the duck, drain, and remove any fat from the cavity opening and around the neck. Cut off and discard the parson's nose. Combine the spring onion, ginger, rice wine, salt, Sichuan peppercorns and star anise. Rub the marinade all over the inside and outside of the duck. Place, breast side down, in a bowl with the remaining marinade and leave in the fridge for at least 1 hour. Put the duck and the marinade, breast side up, on a heatproof plate in a steamer, or cut into halves or quarters and put in several steamers.

Steam over simmering water in a covered wok for 1½ hours, replenishing with boiling water during cooking. Remove the duck, discard the marinade,

and let cool. Rub the soy sauce over the duck and then dredge in the cornflour, pressing lightly to make it adhere to the skin. Let the duck dry in the fridge for several hours until very dry.

Fill a wok one-quarter full of oil. Heat the oil to 190°C (375°F), or until a piece of bread fries golden brown in 10 seconds when dropped in the oil. Lower the duck into the oil and fry, ladling the oil over the top, until the skin is crisp and golden.

Drain the duck and, using a cleaver, cut the duck through the bones into pieces. Serve plain or with hoisin sauce and pancakes or bread.

SERVES 4

Right: Steaming the duck and then frying it keeps the meat very moist and allows the marinade flavours to penetrate.

Far right: For serving, poultry is traditionally chopped into bite-size pieces, rather than jointed, so that the pieces can be picked up with chopsticks.

卤水鸡

Soy Chicken

1.5 kg (3 lb 5 oz) chicken
1 tablespoon ground Sichuan peppercorns
2 tablespoons grated ginger
2 tablespoons sugar
3 tablespoons Shaoxing rice wine
310 ml (10¾ fl oz/1¼ cups) dark soy sauce

185 ml (6 fl oz/¾ cup) light soy sauce
625 ml (21½ fl oz/2½ cups) oil
440 ml (15¼ fl oz/1¾ cups) chicken and meat stock
  (page 181)
2 teaspoons roasted sesame oil

Rinse the chicken, drain, and remove any fat from the cavity opening and around the neck. Cut off and discard the parson's nose. Rub the Sichuan peppercorns and ginger all over the inside and outside of the chicken. Combine the sugar, rice wine and soy sauces, add the chicken and marinate in the fridge for at least 3 hours, turning occasionally.

Heat a wok over high heat, add the oil and heat until very hot. Drain the chicken, reserving the marinade, and fry for 8 minutes until browned. Put in a clay pot or casserole with the marinade and stock. Bring to the boil, then simmer, covered, for 35–40 minutes. Leave off the heat for 2–3 hours, transferring to the fridge once cool. Drain the chicken, brush with oil and refrigerate for 1 hour.

Using a cleaver, chop the chicken through the bones into bite-size pieces, pour over a couple of tablespoons of sauce and serve.

The sauce can be reused as a 'Master Sauce' (see page 187).

SERVES 6

The soy sauce and sugar in the marinade turn the chicken skin a rich dark brown when cooked.

京蔥炒牛肉

Stir-fried Beef with Spring Onions

This Northern dish combines deliciously tender beef with a glaze of soy sauce and sugar and fried spring onions (scallions). You can serve it with Mandarin pancakes or rice.

500 g (1 lb 2 oz) rump or sirloin steak
2 garlic cloves, finely chopped
2 tablespoons light soy sauce
1 tablespoon Shaoxing rice wine
2 teaspoons sugar
1 tablespoon cornflour (cornstarch)
3 tablespoons oil
5 spring onions (scallions), green part only,
    cut into thin strips

SAUCE
3 tablespoons light soy sauce
2 teaspoons sugar
½ teaspoon roasted sesame oil

Cut the beef across the grain into 2 mm (⅛ inch) thick slices, then cut into bite-size pieces. Combine with the garlic, soy, rice wine, sugar and cornflour. Marinate in the fridge for at least 1 hour. Drain.

To make the sauce, combine all the ingredients.

Heat a wok over high heat, add the oil and heat until very hot. Cook the beef in two batches for 1½ minutes, or until brown. Remove and drain. Pour the oil from the wok, leaving 1 tablespoon.

Reheat the reserved oil over high heat until very hot and stir-fry the spring onion for 1 minute. Add the beef and the sauce. Toss to coat the meat and spring onion with the sauce.

SERVES 6

酸甜红烧排骨

Spareribs with Sweet-and-Sour Sauce

This delicious dish is Cantonese in origin. The sauce should be bright and translucent, the meat tender and succulent, and the flavour neither too sweet nor too sour. If you prefer you can use a boneless cut of pork such as loin.

500 g (1 lb 2 oz) Chinese-style pork spareribs
¼ teaspoon salt
¼ teaspoon freshly ground black pepper
1 teaspoon sugar
1 tablespoon Chinese spirit (Mou Tai) or brandy
1 egg yolk, beaten
1 tablespoon cornflour (cornstarch)
oil for deep-frying

SAUCE
1 tablespoon oil
1 small green capsicum (pepper), shredded
3 tablespoons sugar
2 tablespoons clear rice vinegar
1 tablespoon light soy sauce
1 tablespoon tomato paste (purée)
¼ teaspoon roasted sesame oil
2½ tablespoons chicken and meat stock (page 181)
2 teaspoons cornflour (cornstarch)

Ask the butcher to cut the slab of spareribs crosswise into thirds that measure 5 cm (2 inches) in length, or use a cleaver to do so yourself. Cut the ribs between the bones to separate them. Put the pieces in a bowl with the salt, pepper, sugar and Chinese spirit. Marinate in the fridge for at least 35 minutes, turning occasionally.

Meanwhile, blend the egg yolk with the cornflour and enough water to make a thin batter. Remove the spareribs from the marinade and coat them with the batter.

Fill a wok one-quarter full of oil. Heat the oil to 180°C (350°F), or until a piece of bread fries golden brown in 15 seconds when dropped in

the oil. Fry the spareribs in batches for 5 minutes until they are crisp and golden, stirring to separate them, then remove and drain. Reheat the oil and fry the spareribs again for 1 minute to darken their colour. Remove and drain well on crumpled paper towels. Keep warm in a low oven.

To make the sauce, heat a wok over high heat, add the oil and heat until very hot. Stir-fry the green capsicum for a few seconds, then add the sugar, rice vinegar, soy sauce, tomato paste, sesame oil and stock, and bring to the boil. Combine the cornflour with enough water to make a paste, add to the sauce and simmer until thickened. Add the spareribs and toss to coat them with the sauce. Serve hot.

SERVES 4

Chapter 5

VEGETABLE DISHES

Chinese vegetarian food is not always quite what it seems. The Chinese are not great meat eaters and vegetables predominate, particularly the glorious varieties of Chinese greens. However, despite appearances this is not vegetarian food. The dishes are invariably cooked in a chicken stock, flavoured with fish and oyster sauces or fried in animal oil.

豆腐菠菜汤

Tofu and Spinach Soup

This simple but beautiful soup is also known as 'emerald and white jade soup' in Chinese. It is a clear soup, which requires a very good stock for flavour.

120 g (4 oz) soft tofu, drained
100 g (3½ oz) baby English spinach leaves

1 litre (35 fl oz/4 cups) chicken and meat stock
  (page 181)
1 tablespoon light soy sauce

Cut the tofu into slices about 5 mm (¼ inch) thick. Roughly chop any large baby spinach leaves.

Bring the stock to a rolling boil in a large clay pot or saucepan, then add the tofu slices and soy sauce.

Return to the boil, then reduce the heat and simmer gently for 2 minutes. Skim any scum from the surface. Add the spinach and cook for 1–2 minutes. Season with salt and white pepper. Serve hot.

PICTURE ON OPPOSITE PAGE

SERVES 4

番茄蛋花汤

Tomato and Egg Soup

This delicious and nutritious soup is simplicity itself and is sometimes known as an egg drop soup because the egg is slowly poured in near the end of cooking.

250 g (9 oz) firm ripe tomatoes
2 eggs
1 spring onion (scallion), finely chopped
1 tablespoon oil

1 litre (35 fl oz/4 cups) vegetable or chicken and meat stock (page 181)
1 tablespoon light soy sauce
1 tablespoon cornflour (cornstarch)

Score a cross in the bottom of each tomato. Plunge into boiling water for 20 seconds, then drain and peel the skin away from the cross. Cut into slices or thin wedges, trimming off the core. Beat the eggs with a pinch of salt and a few pieces of spring onion.

Heat a wok over high heat, add the oil and heat until very hot. Stir-fry the spring onion for a few seconds to flavour the oil, then pour in the stock and bring to the boil. Add the tomato and return to the boil. Add the soy sauce and very slowly pour in the beaten eggs, stirring as you pour. Return to the boil.

Combine the cornflour with enough water to make a paste, add to the soup and simmer until thickened.

SERVES 4

炒双冬

Stir-fried Twin Winter

This simple dish is called 'twin winter' because both mushrooms and bamboo shoots are at their best in the winter months. Another version of this dish, triple winter, uses bamboo shoots and mushrooms with cabbage.

12 dried Chinese mushrooms
300 g (10½ oz) fresh or tinned bamboo shoots, rinsed and drained
3 tablespoons oil

2 tablespoons light soy sauce
2 teaspoons sugar
2 teaspoons cornflour (cornstarch)
½ teaspoon roasted sesame oil

Soak the dried mushrooms in boiling water for 30 minutes, then drain, reserving the liquid, and squeeze out any excess water. Remove and discard the stems and cut the caps in half (or quarters if large). Cut the bamboo shoots into small pieces the same size as the mushrooms.

Heat a wok over high heat, add the oil and heat until very hot. Stir-fry the mushrooms and bamboo shoots for 1 minute. Add the soy sauce

and sugar, stir a few times, then add 125 ml (4 fl oz/½ cup) of the reserved liquid. Bring to the boil and braise for 2 minutes, stirring constantly.

Combine the cornflour with enough water to make a paste, add to the sauce and simmer until thickened. Sprinkle with the sesame oil, blend well and serve.

SERVES 4

蚝油炒芥蘭

Chinese Broccoli in Oyster Sauce

Chinese broccoli differs from its Western relative in that the stems are long, the florets are tiny, and the flavour is slightly bitter. Some versions are purple. Chinese broccoli is available in Chinese grocers.

1 kg (2 lb 4 oz) Chinese broccoli (gai lan)
1½ tablespoons oil
2 spring onions (scallions), chopped
1½ tablespoons grated ginger
3 garlic cloves, finely chopped
3 tablespoons oyster sauce

1½ tablespoons light soy sauce
1 tablespoon Shaoxing rice wine
1 teaspoon sugar
1 teaspoon roasted sesame oil
125 ml (4 fl oz/½ cup) chicken stock (page 181)
2 teaspoons cornflour (cornstarch)

Wash the broccoli well. Discard any tough stems and diagonally cut into 2 cm (¾ inch) pieces through the stem and the leaf. Blanch the broccoli in a pan of boiling water for 2 minutes, or until the stems and leaves are just tender, then refresh in cold water and dry thoroughly.

Heat a wok over high heat, add the oil and heat until very hot. Stir-fry the spring onion, ginger and garlic for 10 seconds, or until fragrant. Add the broccoli and cook until the broccoli is heated through. Combine the remaining ingredients, add to the wok, stirring until the sauce has thickened, and toss to coat the broccoli.

SERVES 6

北方豆腐

Northern–style Tofu

This dish was apparently a favourite of Dowager Empress Tzu-Hsi in the nineteenth century, and it's still a popular classic in China today. The tofu is first fried, then simmered so that it melts in your mouth.

1 kg (2 lb 4 oz) firm tofu, drained
oil for deep-frying
125 g (4½ oz/1 cup) cornflour (cornstarch)
2 eggs, lightly beaten
1 tablespoon finely chopped ginger
330 ml (11¼ fl oz/1⅓ cups) chicken stock (page 181)

2 tablespoons Shaoxing rice wine
1 teaspoon salt, or to taste
½ teaspoon sugar
1½ teaspoons roasted sesame oil
2 spring onions (scallions), green part only, finely
  chopped

Holding a cleaver parallel to the cutting surface, slice each tofu cake in half horizontally. Cut each piece into 3 cm (1¼ inch) squares.

Fill a wok one-quarter full of oil. Heat the oil to 190°C (375°F), or until a piece of bread fries golden brown in 10 seconds when dropped in the oil. Coat each piece of tofu in the cornflour, then dip in the beaten egg to coat. Cook the tofu in batches for 3–4 minutes on each side, or until golden brown. Remove with a wire sieve or slotted spoon and drain in a colander. Pour the oil from the wok, leaving 1 teaspoon.

Reheat the reserved oil over high heat until very hot and stir-fry the ginger for 5 seconds, or until fragrant. Add the stock, rice wine, salt and sugar, and bring to the boil. Add the fried tofu and pierce the pieces with a fork so that they will absorb the cooking liquid. Cook over medium heat for 20 minutes, or until all the liquid is absorbed. Drizzle the sesame oil over the tofu, toss carefully to coat, sprinkle with the spring onion and serve.

SERVES 6

Double-cooked Yard-long Beans

This Sichuanese recipe is so named because the beans, after being fried until tender, are then cooked again with seasonings and a sauce. Traditionally yard-long, or snake, beans are used. These are available in Chinese shops, but French beans are equally delicious.

1 kg (2 lb 4 oz) yard-long (snake) beans or French beans, trimmed
150 g (5½ oz) minced (ground) pork or beef
2 tablespoons light soy sauce
1½ tablespoons Shaoxing rice wine
½ teaspoon roasted sesame oil

oil for deep-frying
5 tablespoons finely chopped preserved mustard cabbage
3 spring onions (scallions), finely chopped
1½ teaspoons sugar

Diagonally cut the beans into 5 cm (2 inch) pieces. Lightly chop the meat with a cleaver until it goes slightly fluffy. Put the meat in a bowl, add 1 teaspoon of the soy sauce, 1 teaspoon of the rice wine and the sesame oil and stir vigorously to combine.

Fill a wok one-quarter full of oil. Heat the oil to 180°C (350°F), or until a piece of bread fries golden brown in 15 seconds when dropped in the oil. Add a third of the beans, covering the wok with the lid as they are placed in the oil to prevent the oil from splashing. Cook for 3½–4 minutes, stirring constantly, until they are tender and golden brown at the edges. Remove with a wire

sieve or slotted spoon and drain. Reheat the oil and repeat with the remaining beans. Pour the oil from the wok, leaving 1 tablespoon.

Reheat the reserved oil over high heat until very hot, add the meat and stir-fry until the colour changes, mashing and chopping to separate the pieces of meat. Push the meat to the side and add the preserved mustard cabbage and spring onion. Stir-fry over high heat for 15 seconds, or until fragrant. Add the beans with the remaining soy sauce and rice wine, sugar and 1 tablespoon water, and return the meat to the centre of the pan. Toss lightly to coat the beans with the sauce.

SERVES 6

佛跳墙

Buddha's Delight

The original recipe for this well-known vegetarian dish used no less than eighteen different ingredients to represent the eighteen buddhas. Nowadays, anything between six to eight ingredients is usual practice.

25 g (1 oz) tiger lily buds (golden needles)
6–8 dried Chinese mushrooms
10 g (¼ oz/1 cup) dried black fungus (wood ears)
150 g (5½ oz) braised gluten or ready-made braised
    gluten, drained
50 g (1¾ oz) tofu puffs (deep-fried cubes of tofu)
100 g (3½ oz/1 cup) bean sprouts
1 carrot

4 tablespoons oil
50 g (1¾ oz/½ cup) snowpeas (mangetout), ends
    trimmed
1 teaspoon salt
½ teaspoon sugar
4 tablespoons vegetable stock (page 180)
2 tablespoons light soy sauce
½ teaspoon roasted sesame oil

Soak the tiger lily buds in boiling water for 30 minutes. Rinse and drain the tiger lily buds, and trim off any roots if they are hard. Soak the dried mushrooms in boiling water for 30 minutes, then drain and squeeze out any excess water. Remove and discard the stems and cut the caps in half (or quarters if large). Soak the dried black fungus in cold water for 20 minutes, then drain and squeeze out any excess water. Cut any large pieces of fungus in half.

Cut the gluten and tofu into small pieces. Wash the bean sprouts, discarding any husks and straggly end pieces, and dry thoroughly. Diagonally cut the carrot into thin slices.

Heat a wok over high heat, add the oil and heat until very hot. Stir-fry the carrot for 30 seconds, then add the snowpeas and bean sprouts. Stir-fry for 1 minute, then add the gluten, tofu, lily buds, mushrooms, black fungus, salt, sugar, stock and soy sauce. Toss everything together, then cover and braise for 2 minutes at a gentle simmer.

Add the sesame oil, toss it through the mixture and serve hot or cold.

SERVES 4

Far left: Tiger lily buds, or golden needles, are dried unopened lilies.

Left: When reconstituted, tiger lily buds resemble limp bean sprouts.

四川腌黄瓜

Sichuan Pickled Cucumber

The complexity of flavours in this simple pickle is unusual. The seasonings combine to create a taste that is simultaneously sweet, sour, hot and numbing.

200 g (7 oz) cucumbers
½ teaspoon salt
30 g (1 oz) ginger, finely shredded
½ small red chilli, seeded and finely shredded
3 tablespoons roasted sesame oil

½ teaspoon Sichuan peppercorns
6 dried chillies, seeded and cut into 5 mm (¼ inch) lengths
1½ tablespoons clear rice vinegar
1½ tablespoons sugar

Cut the cucumbers in half lengthways, remove the seeds, and cut into 6 cm (2½ inch) long, 2 cm (¾ inch) thick slices. Place in a bowl, add the salt, toss lightly and leave for 30 minutes. Soak the ginger in a bowl of cold water for 20 minutes.

Pour off any water that has accumulated with the cucumber, rinse the cucumber lightly, then drain thoroughly and pat dry. Place the cucumber in a bowl with the drained ginger and chilli.

Heat a wok over high heat, add the sesame oil and heat until very hot. Add the peppercorns and stir-fry for 15 seconds until fragrant. Add the dried chilli and stir-fry for 15 seconds, or until dark. Pour into the bowl with the cucumber, toss lightly and leave to cool. Add the vinegar and sugar, toss to coat, then leave in the fridge for at least 6 hours or overnight. Serve cold or at room temperature.

SERVES 6 AS A SNACK

Chapter 6

STREET FOOD

The tradional dai pai dongs are a Hong Kong legend. Pavement restaurants, they trade out of mobile metal carts, flocking to night markets and setting up in busy alleyways. Local food is sold in a similar way all over China. Customers sit outside at a few wobbly tables and can enjoy their favourite noodles, chilli crabs, clams or other dishes.

Steamed Breads

The basic yeast dough can be used to make lots of different steamed buns, called mantou in China. Flower rolls are one of the simplest shapes, while silver thread rolls require more dexterity. These breads are delicious with red-cooked meats.

1 quantity basic yeast dough (page 180)

3 tablespoons roasted sesame oil

Cut the dough in half and, on a lightly floured surface, roll out each half to form a 30 x 10 cm (12 x 4 inch) rectangle. Brush the surface of the rectangles liberally with the sesame oil. Place one rectangle directly on top of the other, with both oiled surfaces facing up. Starting with one of the long edges, roll up the dough swiss-roll style. Pinch the two ends to seal in the sesame oil.

Lightly flatten the roll with the heel of your hand and cut the roll into 5 cm (2 inch) pieces. Using a chopstick, press down on the centre of each roll, holding the chopstick parallel to the cut edges. (This will cause the ends to 'flower' when they are steamed.) Arrange the shaped rolls well apart in four steamers lined with greaseproof paper punched with holes. Cover and let rise for 15 minutes.

Cover and steam each steamer separately over simmering water in a wok for 15 minutes, or until

the rolls are light and springy. Keep the rolls covered until you are about to eat them to make sure they stay soft.

The dough can also be shaped in other ways, one of the most popular being silver thread bread. Divide the dough in half and roll each half into a sausage about 3 cm (1¼ inches) in diameter, then cut each sausage into six pieces. Roll six of the pieces into rectangles 20 x 10 cm (8 x 4 inches) and set aside. Roll the remaining pieces into rectangles 20 x 10 cm (8 x 4 inches), brush each with a little sesame oil and fold in half to a 10 cm (4 inch) square. Brush with more sesame oil and fold in half again. Cut into thin strips crossways. Place one of the rectangles on the work surface and stretch the strips so they fit down the centre. Fold the ends and sides in to completely enclose the strips. Repeat with the remaining dough until you have six loaves. Steam as for the flower rolls for 20–25 minutes.

MAKES 12 FLOWER ROLLS OR 6 SILVER THREAD LOAVES

Folding sesame oil into the dough means that when the breads are steamed, the layers will spring open.

什锦粥

Rainbow Congee

To the Chinese, congee is an extremely versatile dish. It is a favourite comfort food, a dish prepared for convalescents because it is so soothing to eat, filling and flavourful.

220 g (7¾ oz/1 cup) short-grain rice
2 dried Chinese mushrooms
80 g (3 oz) snowpeas (mangetout), ends trimmed
2 Chinese sausages (lap cheong)
2 tablespoons oil
¼ red onion, finely diced

1 carrot, cut into 1 cm (½ inch) dice
2–2.25 litres (70–79 fl oz/8–9 cups) chicken stock (page 181) or water
¼ teaspoon salt
3 teaspoons light soy sauce

Put the rice in a bowl and, using your fingers as a rake, rinse under cold running water to remove any dust. Drain the rice in a colander.

Soak the dried mushrooms in boiling water for 30 minutes, then drain and squeeze out any excess water. Remove and discard the stems and chop the caps into 5 mm (¼ inch) dice. Cut the snowpeas into 1 cm (½ inch) pieces.

Place the sausages on a plate in a steamer. Cover and steam over simmering water in a wok for 10 minutes, then cut them into small pieces.

Heat a wok over medium heat, add the oil and heat until hot. Stir-fry the sausage until it is brown and the fat has melted out of it. Remove with a

wire sieve or slotted spoon and drain. Pour the oil from the wok, leaving 1 tablespoon.

Reheat the reserved oil over high heat until very hot. Stir-fry the red onion until soft and transparent. Add the mushrooms and carrot and stir-fry for 1 minute, or until fragrant.

Put the mushroom mixture in a clay pot, casserole or saucepan and stir in 2 litres (70 fl oz/8 cups) stock, the salt, soy sauce and the rice. Bring to the boil, then reduce the heat and simmer very gently, stirring occasionally, for 1¾–2 hours, or until it has a porridge-like texture and the rice is breaking up. If it is too thick, add any leftover stock and return to the boil. Toss in the snowpeas and sausage, cover and stand for 5 minutes before serving.

SERVES 6

叉烧汤面

Char Siu Noodle Soup

Noodles in soup are far more popular than fried noodles (chow mein) in China. Like fried rice, noodle dishes are eaten as snacks rather than served as part of an everyday meal. This is a basic recipe—you can use different ingredients for the topping.

4 dried Chinese mushrooms
200 g (7 oz) barbecue pork (char siu)
100 g (3½ oz/⅓ cup) fresh or tinned bamboo shoots, rinsed
100 g (3½ oz) green vegetable, such as English spinach, bok choy (pak choi) or Chinese cabbage
2 spring onions (scallions)
450 g (1 lb) fresh or 350 g (12 oz) dried egg noodles

1 litre (35 fl oz/4 cups) chicken and meat stock (page 181)
2–3 tablespoons oil
1 teaspoon salt
½ teaspoon sugar
1 tablespoon light soy sauce
1 teaspoon Shaoxing rice wine
¼ teaspoon roasted sesame oil

Soak the dried mushrooms in boiling water for 30 minutes, then drain and squeeze out any excess water. Remove and discard the stems and shred the caps. Thinly shred the pork, bamboo shoots, green vegetable and spring onions.

Cook the noodles in a pan of salted boiling water for 2–3 minutes if fresh and 10 minutes if dried, then drain and place in four bowls. Bring the stock to the boil, then reduce the heat to simmering.

Heat a wok over high heat, add the oil and heat until very hot. Stir-fry the pork and half the spring onion for 1 minute, then add the mushrooms, bamboo shoots and green vegetable and stir-fry for 1 minute. Add the salt, sugar, soy sauce, rice wine and sesame oil and blend well.

Pour the stock over the noodles and top with the meat mixture and the remaining spring onion.

SERVES 4

炯鸡翅

Braised Chicken Wings

The Chinese love to eat every part of the chicken and the wings, deep-fried and crisp, are a favourite snack. This recipe is a simple one that makes a good snack or first course. You'll need to hand out finger bowls.

24 chicken wings
3 lumps rock (lump) sugar
1 tablespoon dark soy sauce
1 tablespoon light soy sauce
1 tablespoon Shaoxing rice wine

oil for deep-frying
2 teaspoons finely chopped ginger
1 spring onion (scallion), finely chopped
2 tablespoons hoisin sauce
125 ml (4 fl oz/½ cup) chicken stock (page 181)

Discard the tip of each chicken wing. Cut each wing into two pieces through the joint. Put the wing pieces in a bowl.

Put the rock sugar, dark soy sauce, light soy sauce and rice wine in a small jug. Mix until combined, breaking the sugar down as much as you can. Pour the mixture over the chicken wings, then marinate in the fridge for at least 1 hour, or overnight.

Drain the chicken wings, reserving the marinade. Fill a wok one-quarter full of oil. Heat the oil to 180°C (350°F), or until a piece of bread fries golden brown in 15 seconds when dropped in the oil. Cook the chicken wings in batches for 2–3 minutes, or until they are well browned.

Drain on paper towels.

Carefully pour the oil from the wok, reserving 1 tablespoon. Reheat the wok over high heat, add the reserved oil and heat until very hot. Stir-fry the ginger and spring onion for 1 minute. Add the hoisin sauce, reserved marinade and chicken wings and cook for 1 minute, then add the stock and bring to the boil. Reduce the heat, cover the wok and cook gently for 8–10 minutes, or until the chicken wings are cooked through and tender.

Increase the heat and bring the sauce to the boil, uncovered. Cook until the sauce reduces to a sticky coating.

SERVES 6

Spring Onion Pancakes

One of the most popular snacks in Northern China is crisp, spring onion pancakes eaten straight from the hot oil. Some restaurants also make big, thick ones that they cut into wedges and serve as an accompaniment to a meal.

250 g (9 oz/2 cups) plain (all-purpose) flour
½ teaspoon salt
1 tablespoon oil
3 tablespoons roasted sesame oil

2 spring onions (scallions), green part only,
  finely chopped
oil for frying

Place the flour and salt in a mixing bowl and stir to combine. Add the oil and 220 ml (8 fl oz/ ⅞ cup) boiling water and, using a wooden spoon, mix to a rough dough. Turn the dough out onto a lightly floured surface and knead for 5 minutes, or until smooth and elastic. If the dough is very sticky, knead in a little more flour. Cover the dough with a cloth and let it rest for 20 minutes.

On a lightly floured surface, use your hands to roll the dough into a long roll. Divide the dough into 24 pieces. Working with one portion of dough at a time, place the dough, cut edge down, on the work surface. Using a small rolling pin, roll it out to a 10 cm (4 inch) circle. Brush the surface generously with the sesame oil and sprinkle with some spring onion. Starting with the edge closest to you, roll up the dough and pinch the ends to seal in the spring onion and sesame oil. Lightly flatten the roll, then roll it up again from one end like a snail, pinching the end to seal it. Repeat with the remaining dough, sesame oil and spring onion. Let the rolls rest for 20 minutes.

Place each roll flat on the work surface and press down with the palm of your hand. Roll out to a 10 cm (4 inch) circle and place on a lightly floured tray. Stack the pancakes between lightly floured sheets of baking paper and leave for 20 minutes.

Heat a frying pan over medium heat, brush the surface with oil, and add two or three of the pancakes at a time. Cook for 2–3 minutes on each side, turning once, until the pancakes are light golden brown and crisp. Remove and drain on paper towels. Serve immediately.

MAKES 24

Spread the spring onion (scallion) through the dough by first rolling up the pancake and spring onion, then rolling this into a snail shape, and finally by rolling the snail into a pancake again.

叉烧

Char Siu

Char siu, or barbecue pork, is a Cantonese speciality that can be seen hanging in Chinese restaurants. Char siu means 'suspended over fire' and is traditionally dyed a red colour.

MARINADE
1 tablespoon rock (lump) sugar
1 tablespoon yellow bean sauce
1 tablespoon hoisin sauce
1 tablespoon oyster sauce
1 tablespoon red fermented tofu
1 tablespoon Chinese spirit
  (Mou Tai) or brandy
½ teaspoon roasted sesame oil

750 g (1 lb 10 oz) centre-cut pork loin, trimmed and cut
  into four 20 cm (8 inch) strips
2 tablespoons maltose or honey, dissolved with a
  little water

To make the marinade, combine the ingredients. Add the pork to the marinade and leave in the fridge for at least 6 hours.

Preheat the oven to 220°C (425°F). Put a baking dish with 600 ml (21½ fl oz/2½ cups) boiling water in the bottom of the oven. Drain the pork, reserving the marinade. Put an S-shaped meat hook through one end of each strip and hang from the top rack.

Cook for 10–15 minutes, then baste with the marinade. Reduce the heat to 180°C (350°F) and

cook for 8–10 minutes. Cool for 2–3 minutes, then brush with the maltose and lightly brown under a grill (broiler) for 4–5 minutes, turning to give a charred look around the edges.

Cut the meat into slices. Add 185 ml (6 fl oz/ ¾ cup) cooking liquid to the marinade. Bring to the boil and cook for 2 minutes. Strain and pour over the pork.

SERVES 4

Hanging the char siu to roast above a tray of water creates a steamy atmosphere which helps keep the meat moist.

Tea Eggs

Tea eggs, braised in a fragrant tea and soy sauce mixture, are easy to make and great for snacks—they can be reheated and taste equally good hot or cold. In China, they are found in tea houses and roadside stalls, often bubbling away in vats full of hot tea.

10 very fresh eggs or 20 quail eggs

TEA COOKING MIXTURE
3 tablespoons light soy sauce
3 tablespoons Shaoxing rice wine

1 star anise
1 tablespoon sugar
1 cinnamon stick
3 slices ginger, smashed with the flat side of a cleaver
3 tablespoons Chinese black tea leaves

Place the eggs in a saucepan with enough cold water to cover. Bring the water to the boil, then reduce the heat to low and let the eggs simmer for 10 minutes, or until they are hard-boiled. Refresh the eggs in cold water. Drain the eggs and lightly tap and roll the shells on a hard surface to crack them. Do not remove the shells.

Put the tea cooking mixture ingredients in a heavy-based clay pot, casserole or saucepan

with 1 litre (35 fl oz/4 cups) water and heat until boiling. Reduce the heat to low and simmer for 20 minutes. Add the cooked eggs and simmer for 45 minutes. Turn off the heat and let the eggs sit in the tea mixture until cool enough to handle. Remove the shells and serve the eggs warm or cold, cut into wedges, with some of the cooking mixture on top.

MAKES 10 EGGS OR 20 QUAIL EGGS

NOODLES

Noodles geographically divide China, from the cool North, where hardy wheat is a staple made into mian— wheat-flour noodles—down to the warm, humid South, where ground rice is turned into rice noodles —fen.

Though both kinds of noodles are now eaten all over China, noodles remain more of a staple in the North than the South, where a bowl of rice is the usual accompaniment to a meal.

Mian is the name for noodles made from wheat and barley, though it is often used as the general name for all noodles across China. They can be dried or fresh, made by machine or hand, and eggs can be added to the flour and water paste to make egg noodles, a Cantonese speciality.

Fen is the Chinese word for the flour made from millet and rice, and also refers to noodles made from ground rice. Popular in the South, they are also known as Sha He noodles after a town near Guangzhou, renowned for the quality of its noodles. Fresh rice noodles are formed in sheets and cut up after steaming to make the soft white noodles often found in dim sum. Dried rice noodles come in various thicknesses, from flat rice sticks to strand-like vermicelli, and are usually machine-made.

Fen also refers to non-grain noodles that are not regarded as 'true' noodles made from a staple ingredient such as wheat or rice. Fen si, or bean thread noodles, are made of mung bean flour, and their translucent appearance is reflected in their English names of cellophane or glass noodles. Gan si are made from pressed tofu.

Noodles are most often served in bowls of soup or as roadside snacks in China, especially in the South, where they are rarely served in restaurants and are considered a home-cooking style dish. In the North, noodles are served with meals, and are also found in small restaurants or stalls dedicated to just a few noodle dishes, where the noodles are often hand-thrown to order, then boiled in large pots.

Noodles are a symbol of longevity in Chinese gastronomy and are sometimes eaten on special occasions. Very long, they are rarely cut, as to do this may bring bad luck.

Most areas of China have a special noodle dish associated with the region. In Beijing, these are la mian, the pulled noodles that are also known as Dragon's whiskers. In Sichuan, crossing-the-bridge noodles and ants climbing trees are favourite dishes, while fried Singapore noodles are actually from Fujian.

蒸米粉卷

Steamed Rice Noodle Rolls

A dim sum favourite, these silky rice noodles can be filled with barbecue pork (char siu), prawns or vegetables. The noodles are sold as a long sheet folded into a roll.

PORK FILLING
350 g (12 oz) barbecue pork (char siu), chopped
3 spring onions (scallions), chopped
2 tablespoons chopped coriander (cilantro)

PRAWN FILLING
250 g (9 oz) small prawns (shrimp)
1 tablespoon oil
3 spring onions (scallions), chopped
2 tablespoons chopped coriander (cilantro)

VEGETABLE FILLING
300 g (11 oz) Chinese broccoli (gai lan)
1 teaspoon light soy sauce
1 teaspoon roasted sesame oil
2 spring onions (scallions), chopped

4 fresh rice noodle rolls
oyster sauce

To make the pork filling, combine the pork with the spring onion and coriander.

To make the prawn filling, peel and devein the prawns. Heat a wok over high heat, add the oil and heat until very hot. Stir-fry the prawns for 1 minute, or until they are pink and cooked through. Season with salt and white pepper. Add the spring onion and coriander and mix well.

To make the vegetable filling, wash the broccoli well. Discard any tough-looking stems and chop the rest. Put on a plate in a steamer, cover and steam over simmering water in a wok for 3 minutes, or until the stems and leaves are just tender. Combine the Chinese broccoli with the soy sauce, sesame oil and spring onion.

Unroll the rice noodle rolls (don't worry if they crack a little at the sides). Trim each one into a neat rectangle about 15 x 18 cm (6 x 7 inches) Divide the filling among the rolls, then re-roll the noodles. Put the rolls on a plate in a large steamer, cover and steam over simmering water in a wok for 5 minutes. Serve the rolls cut into pieces and drizzled with the oyster sauce.

MAKES 4

Far left: Put the filling on the piece of noodle roll closest to you.

Left: Roll up carefully so you don't tear it, keeping the filling tucked inside.

担面

Dan Dan Mian

A common street food snack in Sichuan, this dish is now popular all over the North of China and the recipe varies from stall to stall.

1 tablespoon Sichuan peppercorns
200 g (7 oz) minced (ground) pork
50 g (1¾ oz) preserved turnip, rinsed and finely chopped
2 tablespoons light soy sauce
2 tablespoons oil
2 garlic cloves, crushed
2 tablespoons grated ginger

4 spring onions (scallions), finely chopped
2 tablespoons sesame paste or smooth peanut butter
2 tablespoons light soy sauce
2 teaspoons chilli oil
185 ml (6 fl oz/¾ cup) chicken stock (page 181)
400 g (14 oz) thin wheat flour noodles

Dry-fry the Sichuan peppercorns in a wok or pan until brown and aromatic, then crush lightly. Combine the pork with the preserved turnip and soy sauce and leave to marinate for a few minutes. Heat a wok over high heat, add the oil and heat until very hot. Stir-fry the pork until crisp and browned. Remove and drain well.

Add the garlic, ginger and spring onion to the wok and stir-fry for 30 seconds, then add the sesame paste, soy sauce, chilli oil and stock and simmer for 2 minutes.

Cook the noodles in a pan of salted boiling water for 4–8 minutes, then drain well. Divide among four bowls, ladle the sauce over the noodles, then top with the crispy pork and Sichuan peppercorns.

SERVES 4

什锦面

Rainbow Noodles

This dish of prawns (shrimp), bean sprouts and thin rice noodles is enlivened with a touch of Chinese curry powder. Much milder than its Indian counterpart and similar to five-spice powder, you could use a mild Indian curry powder instead.

225 g (8 oz) prawns (shrimp)
1 tablespoon Shaoxing rice wine
2½ tablespoons finely chopped ginger
1 teaspoon roasted sesame oil
300 g (10½ oz) rice vermicelli
2 leeks, white part only
4 tablespoons oil
1½ tablespoons Chinese curry powder

200 g (7 oz/2¼ cups) bean sprouts
60 ml (2 fl oz/¼ cup) chicken stock
   (page 281) or water
2 tablespoons light soy sauce
1 teaspoon salt
½ teaspoon sugar
½ teaspoon freshly ground black pepper

Peel the prawns, leaving the tails intact. Using a sharp knife, score lengthways along the back and remove the vein. Place in a bowl, add the rice wine, 2 teaspoons of the ginger and the sesame oil, and toss to coat.

Soak the noodles in hot water for 10 minutes, then drain. Cut the leeks into 5 cm (2 inch) lengths and shred finely. Wash well and dry thoroughly.

Heat a wok over high heat, add 1 tablespoon of the oil and heat until very hot. Stir-fry the prawns in batches for 1½ minutes, or until they turn

opaque. Remove with a wire sieve or slotted spoon and drain. Pour off the oil and wipe out the wok.

Reheat the wok over high heat, add the remaining oil and heat until very hot. Stir-fry the curry powder for a few seconds, or until fragrant. Add the leek and remaining ginger and stir-fry for 1½ minutes. Add the bean sprouts and cook for 20 seconds, then add the prawns, stock or water, soy sauce, salt, sugar and pepper, and stir to combine.

Add the noodles and toss until they are cooked through and have absorbed all the sauce. Transfer to a serving dish and serve.

SERVES 4

Won Ton Soup

Won ton literally translated means 'swallowing a cloud'. Won tons are categorised as noodles as they use the same dough as egg noodles.

250 g (9 oz) prawns (shrimp)
80 g (2¾ oz/½ cup) peeled water chestnuts
250 g (9 oz) lean minced (ground) pork
3½ tablespoons light soy sauce
3½ tablespoons Shaoxing rice wine
1½ teaspoons salt
1½ teaspoons roasted sesame oil

½ teaspoon freshly ground black pepper
1 teaspoon finely chopped ginger
1½ tablespoons cornflour (cornstarch)
30 square or round won ton wrappers
1.5 litres (52 fl oz/6 cups) chicken stock (page 181)
450 g (1 lb) English spinach, trimmed (optional)
2 spring onions (scallions), green part only, chopped

Peel and devein the prawns. Place in a tea towel and squeeze out as much moisture as possible. Mince the prawns to a coarse paste using a sharp knife or in a food processor.

Blanch the water chestnuts in boiling water for 1 minute, then refresh in cold water. Drain, pat dry and roughly chop them. Place the prawns, water chestnuts, pork, 2 teaspoons of the soy sauce, 2 teaspoons of the rice wine, ½ teaspoon of the salt, ½ teaspoon of the sesame oil, the black pepper, ginger and cornflour in a mixing bowl. Stir vigorously to combine.

Place a teaspoon of filling in the centre of one won ton wrapper. Brush the edge of the wrapper with a little water, fold in half and then bring the two folded corners together and press firmly. Place the won tons on a cornflour-dusted tray.

Bring a saucepan of water to the boil. Cook the won tons, covered, for 5–6 minutes, or until they have risen to the surface. Using a wire sieve or slotted spoon, remove the won tons and divide them among six bowls.

Place the stock in a saucepan with the remaining soy sauce, rice wine, salt and sesame oil, and bring to the boil. Add the spinach and cook until just wilted. Pour the hot stock over the won tons and sprinkle with the spring onion.

SERVES 6

The easiest way to make the won tons is to shape them in the same way as tortellini.

BASICS

An important step in mastering any cusine is learning the basic recipes and techniques. Straight from the recipe journal, here are the ones no Chinese cook would be without.

Boiled or Steamed Rice

200 g (7 oz/1 cup) white long-grain rice

Put the rice in a bowl and, using your fingers as a rake, rinse under cold running water to remove any dust. Drain the rice in a colander.

To boil the rice, put the rice in a heavy-based saucepan with 420 ml (14½ fl oz/1⅔ cups) water and bring to the boil. Reduce the heat to low and simmer, covered, for 15–18 minutes, or until the water has evaporated and craters appear on the surface.

To steam the rice, spread the rice in a steamer lined with greaseproof paper punched with holes, damp cheesecloth or muslin. Cover and steam over simmering water in a wok for 35–40 minutes, or until tender.

Fluff the rice with a fork to separate the grains. Serve or use as directed.

SERVES 4

Crispy Rice

Crispy rice is a great way to use up leftover rice, although you can make it from scratch, as here. The deep-fried rice is put in the bottom of bowls and a soup such as tomato and egg (page 130) is poured over it to make the rice sizzle.

135 g (4¾ oz/⅔ cup) white long-grain rice

Put the rice in a bowl and, using your fingers as a rake, rinse under cold running water to remove any dust. Drain the rice in a colander.

Put the rice and 200 ml (7 fl oz/¾ cup) water in a heavy-based saucepan and bring to the boil. Reduce the heat to low. Simmer, covered, for 15–18 minutes.

Continue to cook uncovered until the rice has formed a cake that comes loose from the pan. Leave to cool. Tip the cake out and dry completely.

Fill a wok one-quarter full of oil. Heat the oil to 180°C (350°F), or until a piece of bread fries golden brown in 15 seconds when dropped in the oil. Cook the rice cake until it is brown and crisp.

SERVES 4

中式薄餅

Mandarin Pancakes

These thin pancakes are also called duck pancakes and are used for wrapping Peking duck (page 92) and other Northern dishes, such as crispy skin duck (page 121), mu shu pork (page 88) and Mongolian lamb (page 95).

450 g (1 lb) plain (all-purpose) flour
310 ml (10¾ fl oz/1¼ cups) boiling water

1 teaspoon oil
roasted sesame oil

Sift the flour into a bowl, slowly pour in the boiling water, stirring as you pour, then add the oil and knead into a firm dough. Cover with a damp tea towel and set aside for 30 minutes.

Turn the dough out onto a lightly floured surface and knead for 8–10 minutes, or until smooth. Divide the dough into three equal portions, roll each portion into a long cylinder, then cut each cylinder into 8 to 10 pieces.

Roll each piece of dough into a ball and press into a flat disc with the palm of your hand. Brush one disc with a little sesame oil and put another disc on top. Using a rolling pin, flatten each pair of discs into a 15 cm (6 inch) pancake.

Heat an ungreased wok or frying pan over high heat, then reduce the heat to low and place the pairs of pancakes, one at a time, in the pan. Turn over when brown spots appear on the underside. When the second side is cooked, lift the pancakes out and carefully peel them apart. Fold each pancake in half with the cooked side facing inwards, and set aside under a damp cloth.

Just before serving, put the pancakes on a plate in a steamer. Cover and steam over simmering water in a wok for 10 minutes.

To store the pancakes, put them in the fridge for 2 days or in the freezer for several months. Reheat the pancakes either in a steamer for 4–5 minutes or a microwave for 30–40 seconds.

MAKES 24–30

Basic Yeast Dough

3 tablespoons sugar
250 ml (9 fl oz/1 cup) warm water
1½ teaspoons dried yeast or 10 g (¼ oz) fresh yeast

400 g (14 oz/3¼ cups) plain (all-purpose) flour
2 tablespoons oil
1½ teaspoons baking powder

Dissolve the sugar in the water, then add the yeast. Stir lightly, then set aside for 10 minutes, or until foamy.

Sift the flour into a bowl and add the yeast mixture and the oil. Using a wooden spoon, mix the ingredients to a rough dough. Turn the mixture out onto a lightly floured surface and knead for 8–10 minutes, or until the dough is smooth and elastic. If it is very sticky, knead in a little more flour—the dough should be soft. Lightly grease a bowl with the oil. Place the dough in the bowl and turn it so that all sides of the dough are coated. Cover the bowl with a damp cloth and set aside to rise in a draught-free place for 3 hours.

Uncover the dough, punch it down, and turn it out onto a lightly floured surface. If you are not using the dough straight away, cover it with plastic wrap and refrigerate.

When you are ready to use the dough, flatten it and make a well in the centre. Place the baking powder in the well and gather up the edges to enclose the baking powder. Pinch the edges to seal. Lightly knead the dough for several minutes to evenly incorporate the baking powder, which will activate immediately.

Use the prepared dough as directed.

SERVES 4

Vegetable Stock

500 g (1 lb 2 oz) fresh soya bean sprouts
10 dried Chinese mushrooms
6 spring onions (scallions), each tied into a knot (optional)

4 litres (140 fl oz/16 cups) water
3 tablespoons Shaoxing rice wine
2 teaspoons salt

Dry-fry the sprouts in a wok for 3–4 minutes. Place the sprouts, mushrooms, spring onions and water in a stockpot and bring to the boil. Reduce the heat and simmer for 1 hour.

Strain through a fine strainer, removing the solids (keep the mushrooms for another use). Return to the pot with the rice wine and salt. Bring to the boil and simmer for 3–4 minutes. Store in the fridge for up to 3 days or freeze in small portions.

MAKES 3 LITRES (105 FL OZ/12 CUPS)

Chicken Stock

1.5 kg (3 lb 5 oz) chicken carcasses, necks, pinions
  and feet
250 ml (9 fl oz/1 cup) Shaoxing rice wine
6 slices ginger, smashed with the flat side of a cleaver

6 spring onions (scallions), ends trimmed, smashed with
  the flat side of a cleaver
4 litres (140 fl oz/16 cups) water

Remove any excess fat from the chicken, then chop into large pieces and place in a stockpot with the rice wine, ginger, spring onions and water and bring to the boil. Reduce the heat and simmer gently for 3 hours, skimming the surface to remove any impurities.

Strain through a fine strainer, removing the solids, and skim the surface to remove any fat. If the stock is too weak, reduce it further. Store in the fridge for up to 3 days or freeze in small portions.

MAKES 3 LITRES (105 FL OZ/12 CUPS)

Chicken and Meat Stock

650 g (1 lb 7 oz) chicken carcasses, necks, pinions and
  feet
650 g (1 lb 7 oz) pork spareribs
4 spring onions (scallions), each tied into a knot
12 slices ginger, smashed with the flat side of a cleaver

4 litres (140 fl oz/16 cups) water
80 ml (2½ fl oz/⅓ cup) Shaoxing rice wine
2 teaspoons salt

Remove any excess fat from the chicken and meat, then chop into large pieces and place in a stockpot with the spring onions, ginger and water and bring to the boil. Reduce the heat and simmer gently for 3½–4 hours, skimming the surface to remove any impurities.

Strain through a fine strainer, removing the solids, and skim the surface to remove any fat. Return to the pot with the rice wine and salt. Bring to the boil and simmer for 3–4 minutes. Store in the fridge for up to 3 days or freeze in small portions.

MAKES 3 LITRES (105 FL OZ/12 CUPS)

醬醋辣醬

Soy and Vinegar Dipping Sauce

Simple dipping sauces are served with foods such as steamed dumplings. The addition of vinegar gives a more rounded flavour than using just soy sauce.

125 ml (4 fl oz/½ cup) light soy sauce

3 tablespoons Chinese black rice vinegar

Combine the soy sauce and vinegar with 2 tablespoons water in a small bowl, then divide among individual dipping bowls.

This dipping sauce goes well with jiaozi (page 14) or dim sum like siu mai (page 32).

MAKES 225 ML (7¾ FL OZ/1 CUP)

醬辣芝麻調味醬

Soy, Vinegar and Chilli Dipping Sauce

125 ml (4 fl oz/½ cup) light soy sauce
2 tablespoons Chinese black rice vinegar

2 red chillies, thinly sliced

Combine the soy sauce, vinegar and chilli in a small bowl, then divide among individual dipping bowls. This dipping sauce goes well with jiaozi (page 14)

or dim sum like har gau (page 22) or tofu rolls (page 31).

MAKES 200 ML (7 FL OZ/¾ CUP)

紅醋調味醬

Red Vinegar Dipping Sauce

125 ml (4 fl oz/½ cup) red rice vinegar

3 tablespoons shredded ginger

Combine the rice vinegar, 2½ tablespoons water and the ginger in a small bowl, then divide among

individual dipping bowls. This dipping sauce goes well with jiaozi (page 14).

MAKES 225 ML (7¾ FL OZ /1 CUP)

酱辣芝麻调味酱

Soy, Chilli and Sesame Dipping Sauce

125 ml (4 fl oz/½ cup) light soy sauce
2½ tablespoons chilli oil

1 tablespoon roasted sesame oil
1 spring onion (scallion), finely chopped

Combine the soy sauce, vinegar and chilli in a small bowl, then divide among individual dipping bowls. This dipping sauce goes well with jiaozi (page 14) or dim sum like har gau (page 22) or tofu rolls (page 31).

MAKES 200 ML (7 FL OZ/ ¾ CUP)

辣椒盐和胡椒

Spicy Salt and Pepper

1 tablespoon salt
2 teaspoons ground Sichuan peppercorns

1 teaspoon five-spice powder

Combine the salt, Sichuan peppercorns and five-spice powder. Dry-fry over low heat, stirring constantly for 2–3 minutes, or until aromatic. This mix can be used as an ingredient or as a dipping condiment for roast duck or chicken.

MAKES 2 TABLESPOONS

辣酱

Chilli Sauce

1 kg (2 lb 4 oz) red chillies, stalks removed
3 teaspoons salt

4 tablespoons sugar
170 ml (5½ fl oz/⅔ cup) clear rice vinegar

Put the chillies in a saucepan with 5 tablespoons water, cover and bring to the boil. Cook until the chillies are tender, then add the salt, sugar and vinegar. Blend the mixture to a paste in a blender or food processor, or push through a sieve. Store in the fridge for up to 1 month or freeze in small portions. Use as an ingredient or dipping sauce.

MAKES 400 ML (ABOUT 14 FL OZ/1½ CUPS)

GLOSSARY

ABALONE A single-shelled mollusc that is a delicacy in China. Sometimes available fresh from specialist fish shops, but more often used dried or tinned. Dried abalone needs to be soaked for 6 hours, then simmered for 4. Tinned can be used as it is.

BAMBOO SHOOTS A bamboo is a giant grass and its shoots are a common vegetable in China. Fresh shoots are cone-shaped and can contain a toxin called hydrocyanic acid, which is removed by boiling for 5 minutes. The more readily available tinned ones are usually cut into strips and need to be rinsed. Dried or preserved bamboo shoots may also be available. Dried ones should be soaked. Winter shoots are more highly prized than spring shoots as they are more tender. Bamboo is known as 'winter' in many dishes.

BARBECUE PORK (CHAR SIU) A Cantonese speciality, these pork pieces are coated in maltose or honey and roasted until they have a red, lacquered appearance. Available at Chinese roast meat restaurants.

BEAN SPROUTS These can be sprouted mung or soya beans. Soya bean sprouts are bigger and more robust, but the two are usually interchangeable. Recipes may tell you to remove the straggly ends, but this is not necessary and is for aesthetic reasons. You can keep the sprouts in water in the fridge for several days. Change the water daily.

BEAN THREAD NOODLES Not true noodles, these are made from mung bean starch and are also labelled as cellophane or glass noodles. They come as vermicelli or slightly thicker strands and need to be soaked. They have no flavour of their own but soak up flavourings they are cooked with.

BITTER MELON Also known as a warty melon, this looks like a pale-green cucumber covered in a warty skin. The flesh is very bitter and needs to be blanched or degorged, then married with strong flavours.

BLACK FUNGUS Also known as wood or cloud ears, this is a cultivated wood fungus, which is dried in pieces and can be found in bags in Chinese shops. When reconstituted, it expands to up to five times its original size. It is used in recipes for both its colour and slightly crunchy, rubbery texture.

BOK CHOY (PAK CHOI) Also called a little Chinese white cabbage, this is a mild, open-leaved cabbage with a fat white or pale-green stem and dark-green leaves. A smaller variety is called Shanghai or baby bok choy. Bok choy is widely available.

CASSIA The bark of the cassia tree is similar to cinnamon, which can be used instead, though cassia has a more woody flavour. It is used as a flavouring, especially in braises.

CHILLI bean paste (toban jiang) Made from broad beans fermented with chillies and salt to give a browny-red sauce, this is an important ingredient in Sichuan cooking, but is never served as a dipping sauce. Other pastes, called hot or Sichuan bean pastes, can be substituted. These are made of fermented soya beans and sometimes other ingredients such as garlic. It is hard to judge their heat, so take care when adding a new one to a recipe. Chinese shops usually have a large number to choose from.

CHILLI OIL A condiment made by pouring smoking hot oil over chilli flakes and seeds. Ready-made versions can be bought.

CHILLI SAUCE Made from fresh chillies and a variety of other ingredients, such as garlic and vinegar, the thicker version is good for cooking and the thinner for a dipping sauce.

CHINESE BROCCOLI (GAI LAN) This has dark-green stalks and leaves and tiny florets.

CHINESE CABBAGE A white cabbage also known as Chinese leaf; Tianjin, Beijing or napa cabbage; or wong bok. There are two main types: one is long with pale-green leaves and a thick white stem, while the other is pale yellow with curlier leaves and a rounder shape. Both are widely available.

CHINESE CHIVES Garlic chives have a long, flat leaf and are green and very garlicky, or yellow with a milder taste. Flowering chives are round-stemmed with a flower at the top, which can be eaten. Both are used as a vegetable rather than as a herb.

CHINESE CURRY POWDER A strong and spicy version of five-spice powder, with additional spices including turmeric and coriander, which lend the curry flavour.

CHINESE HAM A salted and smoked ham with a strong flavour and dryish flesh. Yunnan and Jinhua hams are the best known, and outside China, Yunnan ham can be bought in tins. You can substitute prosciutto if you can't find it.

CHINESE MUSHROOMS The fresh version, found as shiitake mushrooms, is cultivated by the Japanese. The Chinese, however, usually use dried ones, which have a strong flavour and aroma and need to be soaked to reconstitute them before they are used. The soaking liquid can be used to add flavour to dishes. These are widely available.

CHINESE PICKLES These can be made from several types of vegetables, preserved in a clear brine solution or in a soy-based solution, which is called jiang cai. Both can be used where Chinese pickles are called for in a recipe. They are available in packets and jars from Chinese shops.

CHINESE SAUSAGE There are two kinds of Chinese sausage: a red variety, lap cheong or la chang, which is made from pork and pork fat and dried; and a brown variety, yun cheung or xiang chang, which is made from liver and pork and also dried. Chinese sausages have to be cooked before eating.

CHINESE SHRIMP PASTE Very pungent pulverised shrimp. Refrigerate after opening.

CHINESE SPIRITS Distilled from grains, these vary in strength but generally are stronger than Western spirits. Spirits are used for drinking and cooking and Mou Tai is a common brand. Brandy can be substituted.

CHINESE STYLE PORK SPARERIBS These are the shorter, fatter ribs known as pai gwat and are cut into short lengths. If they are unavailable, use any spareribs but trim off any excess fat.

CHINESE TURNIP Looking like a huge white carrot, this is actually a type of radish and is also called Chinese white radish. It has a crisp, juicy flesh and mild radish flavour. It is also known as mooli, or by the Japanese name daikon, and is widely available.

CHOY SUM A green vegetable with tender pale-green stalks, small yellow flowers and dark-green leaves. It has a mild flavour and is often just blanched and eaten with a simple flavouring like garlic or oyster sauce.

CLAY POT Also known as a sand pot, these earthen-ware, lidded pots are used for braises, soups and rice dishes that need to be cooked slowly on the stove. The pots come in different shapes: the squatter ones are for braising and the taller ones for soups and rice. The pots can be fragile and should be heated slowly, preferably with a liquid inside.

CLEAVER A large, oblong, flat-bladed knife. In China, different cleavers are used for all chopping and cutting, but heavy-duty ones are good for chopping through bones as they are very robust. They can be bought in Chinese shops and at kitchenware shops.

DANG GUI A bitter Chinese herb that is a relation of European Angelica and is valued for its medicinal properties. It can be found in Chinese shops or herbalists and looks like small bleached pieces of wood. It is generally added to braises or soups.

DRIED SCALLOPS (CONPOY) Scallops dried to thick amber discs. They need to be soaked or steamed until soft and are often shredded before use. They have a strong flavour so you don't need many, and as they are expensive they are mostly eaten at banquets.

DRIED SHRIMPS These are tiny, orange, saltwater shrimps that have been dried in the sun. They come in different sizes and the really small ones have their heads and shells still attached. Dried shrimp need to be soaked in water or rice wine to soften them before use and are used as a seasoning.

DUMPLING WRAPPERS Used for jiaozi, wheat wrappers, also called Shanghai wrappers or wheat dumpling skins, are white and can be round or square. Egg wrappers for siu mai are yellow and may also be round or square. They are sometimes labelled gow gee wrappers or egg dumpling skins. All are found in the refrigerated cabinets in Chinese shops and good supermarkets and can be frozen until needed.

FERMENTED TOFU A marinated tofu that is either red, coloured with red rice, or white, and may also be flavoured with chilli. It is sometimes called preserved tofu or tofu cheese and is used as a condiment or flavouring. It is sold in jars in Chinese shops.

FIVE-SPICE POWDER A Chinese mixed spice generally made with star anise, cassia, Sichuan pepper, fennel seeds and cloves, which gives a balance of sweet, hot and aromatic flavours. Five-spice may also include cardamom, coriander, dried orange peel and ginger. Used ground together as a powder or as whole spices tied in muslin.

FLAT CABBAGE (TAT SOI) Also known as a rosette cabbage, this is a type of bok choy (pak choi). It looks like a giant flower with shiny, dark-green leaves that grow out flat.

GINGKO NUTS These are the nuts of the maidenhair tree. The hard shells are cracked open and the inner nuts soaked to loosen their skins. The nuts are known for their medicinal properties and are one of the eight treasures in dishes like eight-treasure rice. Shelled nuts can be bought in tins in Chinese shops and are easier to use.

GLUTINOUS RICE A short-grain rice that, unlike other rice, cooks to a sticky mass and so is used in dishes where the rice is required to hold together. Glutinous rice is labelled as such and has plump, highly polished and shiny grains. Black or red glutinous rice, used mainly in desserts, is slightly different.

GUILIN CHILLI SAUCE From the southwest of China, this sauce is made from salted, fermented yellow soya beans and chillies. It is used as an ingredient in cooking. If it is unavailable, use a thick chilli sauce instead.

HOISIN SAUCE This sauce is made from salted, yellow soya beans, sugar, vinegar, sesame oil, red rice for colouring and spices such as five-spice or star anise. It is generally used as a dipping sauce, for meat glazes or in barbecue marinades.

JUJUBES Also known as Chinese or red dates, jujubes are an olive-sized dried fruit with a red, wrinkled skin, which are thought to build strength. They need to be soaked and are used in eight-treasure or tonic-type dishes. They are also thought to be lucky because of their red colour.

LONGANS From the same family as lychees, these are round with smooth, buff-coloured skins, translucent sweet flesh and large brown pips. Available fresh, tinned or dried.

LOTUS LEAVES The dried leaves of the lotus, they need to be soaked before use and are used for wrapping up food like sticky rice to hold it together while it is cooking. They are sold in packets in Chinese shops.

LOTUS ROOT The rhizome of the Chinese lotus, the root looks like a string of three cream-coloured sausages, but when cut into it has a beautifully lacy pattern. It is available fresh, which must be washed, tinned or dried. Use the fresh or tinned version as a fresh vegetable and the dried version in braises.

LOTUS SEEDS These seeds from the lotus are considered medicinal and are used in eight-treasure dishes as well as being roasted, salted or candied and eaten as a snack. Lotus seeds are also made into a sweet paste to fill buns and pancakes. Fresh and dried lotus seeds are both available and dried seeds need to be soaked before use.

MALTOSE A sweet liquid of malted grains used to coat Peking duck and barbecued meats. Honey can be used instead.

MASTER SAUCE This is a stock of soy sauce, rice wine, rock (lump) sugar, spring onions (scallions), ginger and star anise. Additional ingredients vary according to the chef. Meat, poultry or fish is cooked in the stock, then the stock is reserved so it matures, taking on the flavours of everything that is cooked in it. The spices are replenished every few times the sauce is used. Master sauce spices can be bought as a mix, or a ready-made liquid version. Freeze between uses.

MEI KUEI LU CHIEW A fragrant spirit known as Rose Dew Liqueur. Made from sorghum and rose petals. It is used in marinades, but brandy can be used instead.

NOODLES Egg noodles come fresh and dried in varying thicknesses. In recipes they are inter-changeable, so choose a brand that you like and buy the thickness appropriate to the dish you are making. Wheat noodles are also available fresh and dried and are interchangeable in recipes. Rice noodles are made from a paste of ground rice and water and can be bought fresh or as dried rice sticks or vermicelli. The fresh noodles are white and can be bought in a roll.

ONE-THOUSAND-YEAR OLD EGGS Also known as one-hundred-year old or century eggs, these are eggs that have been preserved by coating them in a layer of wood ash, slaked lime and then rice husks. The eggs are left to mature for 40 days to give them a blackish-green yolk and amber white. To eat, the coating is scraped off and the shell peeled.

OYSTER SAUCE A fairly recent invention, this is a Cantonese speciality made with oyster extract. Add to dishes at the end of cooking or use as a dipping sauce or marinade.

PEPPER Used as an ingredient rather than as a condiment, most hot dishes were originally flavoured with copious quantities of pepper rather than the chillies used now. White pepper is used rather than black.

PLUM SAUCE This comes in several varieties, with some brands sweeter than others and some adding chilli, ginger or garlic. It is often served with Peking duck rather than the true sauce and is a good dipping sauce.

PRESERVED GINGER Ginger pickled in rice vinegar and sugar, which is typically used for sweet-and-sour dishes. Japanese pickled ginger could be used as a substitute.

PRESERVED MUSTARD CABBAGE Also called Sichuan pickle or preserved vegetables, this is the root of the mustard cabbage preserved in chilli and salt. It is available whole and shredded in jars or tins.

PRESERVED TURNIP This is Chinese turnip, sliced, shredded or grated, and usually preserved in brine. It has a crunchy texture and needs to be rinsed before using.

RED BEAN PASTE Made from crushed adzuki beans and sugar, this sweet paste is used in soups and to fill dumplings and pancakes. There is a richer black version and this can be used instead.

RICE FLOUR This is finely ground rice, often used to make rice noodles. Glutinous rice flour, used for making sweet things, makes a chewier dough.

RICE VINEGAR Made from fermented rice, Chinese vinegars are milder than Western ones. Clear rice vinegar is mainly used for pickles and sweet-and-sour dishes. Red rice vinegar is a mild liquid used as a dipping sauce and served with shark's fin soup. Black rice vinegar is used in braises, especially in northern recipes—Chinkiang (Zhenjiang) vinegar is a good label. Rice vinegars can last indefinitely but may lose their aroma, so buy small bottles. If you can't find them, use cider vinegar instead of clear and balsamic instead of black.

ROASTED SESAME OIL Chinese sesame oil is made from roasted white sesame seeds and is a rich amber liquid, unlike the pale unroasted Middle Eastern sesame oil. Buy small bottles as it loses its aroma quickly. It does not fry well as it smokes at a low temperature, but sprinkle it on food as a seasoning or use it mixed with another oil for stir-frying.

ROCK (LUMP) SUGAR Yellow rock sugar comes as uneven lumps of sugar, which may need to be further crushed before use if very big. It is a pure sugar that gives a clear syrup and makes sauces it is added to shiny and clear. You can use sugar lumps instead.

SALTED, FERMENTED BLACK BEANS Very salty black soya beans that are fermented using the same moulds as are used for making soy sauce. Added to dishes as a flavouring, they must be rinsed before use and are often mashed or crushed. They are available in jars or bags from specialist shops. You can also use a black bean sauce.

SEA CUCUMBER A slug-like sea creature related to the starfish. Always sold dried, it needs to be reconstituted by soaking. It has a gelatinous texture and no flavour.

SESAME PASTE Made from ground, roasted white sesame seeds, this is a fairly dry paste. It is more aromatic than tahini, which can be used instead by mixing it with a little Chinese sesame oil. Black sesame paste is used for sweets like New Year dumplings.

SHAOXING RICE WINE Made from rice, millet, yeast and Shaoxing's local water, this is aged for at least 3 years, then bottled either in glass or decorative earthenware bottles. Several varieties are available. As a drink, rice wine is served warm in small cups. Dry sherry is the best substitute.

SICHUAN PEPPERCORNS Not a true pepper, but the berries of a shrub called the prickly ash. Sichuan pepper, unlike ordinary pepper, has a pungent flavour and the aftertaste, rather than being simply hot, is numbing. The peppercorns should be crushed and dry-roasted to bring out their full flavour.

SLAB SUGAR Dark brown sugar with a caramel flavour sold in a slab. Soft brown sugar can be used instead.

SOY SAUCE Made from fermented soya beans, soy sauce comes in two styles: light soy sauce, which is also known as just soy sauce or superior soy sauce, and is used with fish, poultry and vegetables, and dark soy sauce, which is more commonly used with meats. Chinese soy sauce, unlike Japanese, is not used as a condiment except with Cantonese cuisine. As it is not meant to be a dipping sauce, it is best to mix a tablespoon of dark with two tablespoons of light to get a good flavour for a condiment. It does not last forever so buy small bottles and store it in the fridge.

SOYA BEANS These are oval, pale-green beans. The fresh beans are cooked in their fuzzy pods and served as a snack. The dried beans can be yellow or black, and the yellow ones are used to make soy milk by boiling and then puréeing the beans with water before straining off the milk. Dried soya beans need to be soaked in water overnight.

SPRING ROLL WRAPPERS Also called spring roll skins, these wrappers are made with egg and are a pale or dark yellow. They are found in the refrigerated cabinets of Chinese shops and supermarkets and can be frozen until needed.

STAR ANISE An aromatic ingredient in Chinese cooking, this is a star-shaped dried seed pod containing a flat seed in each point.

STEAMING A method of cooking food in a moist heat to keep it tender and preserve its flavour. Bamboo steamers fit above a saucepan or wok and a 25 cm (10 inch) steamer is the most useful, although you will need a bigger one for cooking whole fish. Use as many as you need, stacked on top of each other, and reverse them halfway through cooking to ensure the cooking is even. Metal steamers are available, but bamboo ones are preferred in China as they absorb the steam, making the food a little drier.

STIR-FRYING A method of cooking in a wok that only uses a little oil and cooks the food evenly and quickly, retaining its colour and texture. Everything to be cooked needs to be prepared beforehand, cut to roughly the same shape, dry and at room temperature. The wok is heated, then the oil added and heated before the ingredients are thrown in. Stir-frying should only take a couple of minutes, the heat should be high and the ingredients continually tossed.

TIGER LILY BUDS Sometimes called golden needles, these aren't from tiger lilies but are the unopened flowers from another type of lily. The buds are bought dried and then soaked. They have an earthy flavour.

TOFU Also known as bean curd, tofu is called doufu in China and it is made by coagulating soya bean milk. The curds are sold in blocks, either soft, firm or pressed, depending on their water content. Keep the blocks in water in the fridge, changing the water frequently, for up to 2 to 3 days. Japanese tofu can be used but the silken variety is softer than Chinese soft tofu. Available at supermarkets.

TOFU PUFFS Deep-fried squares of tofu, crispy on the outside and spongy in the middle. Frying your own tofu will not be the same, but can be substituted. Puffs, sold in Chinese shops, can be frozen.

WATER CHESTNUTS These are the rhizomes of a plant that grows in paddy fields in China. The nut has a dark-brown shell and a crisp white interior. The raw nuts need to be peeled with a knife and blanched, then stored in water. Tinned ones need to be drained and rinsed.

WATER SPINACH Called ong choy in Chinese, this vegetable has long, dark-green pointed leaves and long hollow stems. Often cooked with shrimp paste.

WINTER MELON A very large dark-green gourd or squash that looks like a watermelon. The skin is dark green, often with a white waxy bloom, and the flesh is pale green.

WOK A bowl-shaped cooking vessel that acts as both a frying pan and a saucepan in the Chinese kitchen. To season it, scrub off the layer of machine oil, then heat with 2 tablespoons of oil over low heat for several minutes. Rub the inside with paper towels, changing the paper until it comes out clean. The inside will continue to darken as it is used and only water should be used for cleaning. Use a different wok for steaming, as boiling water will strip off the seasoning.

WON TON WRAPPERS Also called won ton skins, these are square and yellow and slightly larger than dumpling wrappers. They can be frozen until needed.

YARD-LONG BEANS Also called snake or long beans, these are about 40 cm (16 inches) long. The darker green variety has a firmer texture.

YELLOW BEAN SAUCE This is actually brown in colour and made from fermented yellow soya beans, which are sweeter and less salty than black beans, mixed with rice wine and dark brown sugar. It varies in flavour and texture (some have whole beans in them) and is sold under different names—crushed yellow beans, brown bean sauce, ground bean sauce and bean sauce. It is mainly used in Sichuan and Hunan cuisine.

Index

Published in 2015 by Murdoch Books, an imprint of Allen & Unwin

Murdoch Books Australia
83 Alexander Street
Crows Nest NSW 2065
Phone: +61 (0) 2 8425 0100
www.murdochbooks.com.au
info@murdochbooks.com.au

Murdoch Books UK
Erico House, 6th Floor
93–99 Upper Richmond Road
Putney, London SW15 2TG
Phone: +44 (0) 20 8785 5995
www.murdochbooks.co.uk
info@murdochbooks.co.uk

For Corporate Orders & Custom Publishing contact Noel Hammond,
National Business Development Manager, Murdoch Books Australia

Editor: Audra Barclay
Series Design Manager: Sarah Odgers
Design: Ice Cold Publishing
Photography: Alan Benson, Ian Hofstetter, Jason Lowe
Food styling: Sarah de Nardi
Recipes by: Deh-Ta Hsiung, Nina Simonds, Wendy Quisumbing
Production Manager: Mary Bjelobrk

A cataloguing-in-publication entry is available from the catalogue of
the National Library of Australia at nla.gov.au.

ISBN 978 1 743366561 Australia
ISBN 978 1 743366578 UK

A catalogue record for this book is available from the British Library.

Colour reproduction by Pica Digital Overseas Pte Ltd
Printed by 1010 Printing International, China.